To our Alanna,

Thank you for your friendship and your encouragement and inspiration! You are a bright spirit and a beautiful being!

With much Love,

Mike

To our dear friend
Alanas,

Thank you for
your friendship and
your encouragement
and inspiration!
You are a bright
spirit and a
beautiful being!
With much love,

Guided by Spirit

Michael Pedroncelli

GUIDED BY SPIRIT

Copyright © 2019 by Michael Pedroncelli

All rights reserved. No part of this book may be reproduced or transmitted in any form or by any means without written permission from the author.

https://www.facebook.com/mike.pedroncelli
https://www.instagram.com/mikepedroncelli/

Dedication

To my beloved wife Marie, and my dear friend Chittak, who first listened and expressed interest in all these experiences. Then, encouraged me to write them down and share them in this book format. Thank you dear ones!

Contents

Introduction	....	1
Initiation	....	9
Angels on the Bridge	…..	10
Joseph Rael and the Circle of Light Chamber	….	29
Dreams	....	75
Past Lives	....	107
Thomas	…..	111
Life Between Lives	…..	143
Chokrel	…..	181
Closing	....	207

Introduction

Warning: this *might be* a crazy book that defies reason and categorization. I'm not sure. Why am I writing this and sharing it with you? Oh wait, I know. Just like the overarching story in this book, I have been guided by spirit to do this as part of a journey of connection and integration. Mentally, with the rational mind, I can't understand "why" I'm writing this and sharing it. But, intuitively, I *feel* it's important to share this with you even though the mind says "Huh? What?"

I hope the stories within this story will remind you of something you've experienced and maybe something in or about this book will give you permission to give yourself permission to reflect upon and maybe even share your own, similar experiences. Maybe you'll reflect internally and keep it to yourself, or you'll share privately with some close confidants, or maybe you'll share it more widely and you'll reach people you haven't even met in person yet. That's what this book is for me. And who knows – maybe it will inspire or ignite something in you too that will lead to a meaningful shift or even some external action?

These are just a few of all the experiences I could have chosen to share. But I chose these particular ones to create a connecting thread of awakening or "Aha!" moments which combined to have a net effect of moving me from living unconsciously based on cultural conditioning, or egoic identity, across a threshold and into a return to a "truer" self where I am largely free of what I believed I was or what I should have been for such a long stretch of life.

Much of what's in this book cannot be explained with ordinary logic or normal reality. But, taken as a whole, I see this as a process of some greater force of beauty, grace, harmony, and goodness than I could have ever conceived on my own. And even now, I see this process and the connecting thread as something larger than I can comprehend or articulate. I call it being "**Guided by Spirit**".

Many of these experiences are "metaphysical", "mystical", or "non-ordinary" experiences. They could also be called "spiritual" or "religious" experience.

For as long as I can remember, I have been aware and attuned to these kinds of occurrences and experiences but I shied away from talking about them because I was worried about being viewed and judged as "strange" or "unusual". But, over time, I've met many people and read many such stories and had so many of these life experiences that they have led me to now believe they're not so strange or unusual at all. In fact, I believe we all have these experiences and they are almost always guiding us to a return to the truth of who we are as souls.

I noticed that many of the most important experiences and turning points in my life – some of which I recount here in this book – have happened when I didn't understand what was happening at the time, or why I was doing what I was doing. But, I felt the calls to follow these promptings and I surrendered to the possibility that these promptings were the right thing for me to do and that maybe they were even important. Most times I felt I should or even that I must do them. Then, after I followed those calls to pay attention and follow through with unusual situations, I looked back on them and found them to be extraordinary and important in the course of my overall life journey. This book is like that too. I feel pulled to do it, even though my rational mind and my shy, reclusive personality doesn't want to.

Some examples of other promptings like this where I felt guided, but I didn't understand why I felt the way I did at the time, were when I struck out from my parents' household, when I got married, and when I walked away from a successful professional career right at its peak.

I didn't understand why I had to venture beyond my parents' family. But, I knew I did. From age 12, or so, I felt I belonged to something more than the world of my parents, brothers, extended family, and even something bigger than my parents' friends, and communities. I loved them and I loved everything they believed and were involved in. But, it wasn't enough. I felt I had to explore something larger, not only geographically, but also emotionally, philosophically, and spiritually. I had a sense – not a firm idea that I could articulate or identify, just a sense - that my values, morality, and ideals had common ground with my parents, but also significant differences.

From the ages of 12 to 17, or so, I felt completely lost because I thought I "didn't belong" in my parents' family. My image of "who I was" didn't quite match theirs. I couldn't quite get on board with all their ideas and ideals. I didn't really know who I was or what I was about, but I knew there were some significant differences with my parents and I knew I had to go find out what was "out there" so that I would know what was "in here" inside myself. Somehow, at an intuitive level, but without much consciousness, or understanding about it, I knew it was important to explore these commonalities and differences outside the framework of my parent's household, their communities, and their belief system. And I knew I had to go on my own journey to see what these feelings were all about.

I moved out of my parents' household and went to college in a neighboring state. For three years, I mostly studied technical information at a school to earn a degree so I could have a decent paying corporate job in the "real world" when I graduated. But on my own, I also studied comparative religion, philosophy, history from different traditions, psychology, and even parapsychology, metaphysics, and mystical teachings. It was marvelous to explore all this.

I didn't find a job straight out of college so I returned to my parents' household. As always, I was pulled in lots of different directions, but I think one of the strongest reasons I was pulled back to Albuquerque was to reconnect with a girl I knew from childhood. Her name was Marie Yvette Candelaria. Over the years, the girl had grown into a young woman and she now had a young son, Rito Junior. Then it happened again, just like when I felt the urge to leave my parents. I wanted to be involved with Marie, but I felt I was too young to get serious with someone who already had a young child. I didn't feel I was ready to be a parent or caregiving figure to a child yet. It "didn't compute". But, even though I was only 20 or 21 and my mind was saying "no", my intuition was saying "yes". So, I decided to get more involved with, then get married to this intriguing woman and her son, and we did – we got married and started a family.

My logical, rational, culturally conditioned, planning, and thinking mind felt it was "too soon", "I was too young", "we were too different", "it didn't make sense", and "it might not be the best choice I could make". But, my heart, and gut said YES!, you absolutely MUST do this. Maybe biology had a lot to do with it, but I think there was more to it than that. So, I did it anyway. I followed my heart and told my head to "shush". We dated, then got married. I said YES to merging my life with this woman and her son, and it's been the best thing I've ever done in my life. We're still married 34 years later. We're more and more in love every day and every moment, and my relationship with Rob as his Dad is one of the most important and satisfying things to me – more than I could have ever imagined. Rob, is now 41 years old, with 5 kids, and 4 grandkids of his own. Our grandkids and great grandkids are true bright lights for us and we love them like crazy. And, we have two other sons together, David, age 34, and Carlos, 31, who are amazing, and great joys to me in how they have become their own people and continue to grow and create relationships and their own lives that amaze me. David and his wonderful wife, Toby, just had a beautiful baby boy too. Lots of this beauty and grace happened because I followed my heart and instinct, not my mind and thoughts.

Another example of following some larger guiding force happened when I left a career of 29 years, 3 months, and 13 days at a government research institution. (Not that I was counting it like it was a prison sentence, or anything...) I was in my peak earning years and I reached a point where I could carve out any of several plum roles of my choosing in this prestigious organization. I got along well with my cohorts and I was crazy to leave since it wasn't clear to me what I was so eager to get away from, or what I was going into. But, again, I felt an intuitive urge to "move on" to the next phase of my life – whatever that might be. I didn't know how it would work out to walk away, at age 50, from what I had known so well for almost three decades of being a householder and breadwinner and playing the various roles I had in relation to that job. But, I felt "it was time" and "I had to move on."

These are three examples of following a prompting or offer of goodness and greatness that came from something bigger than my own, thinking mind, my social conditioning, and the sum total of what I had learned up to then about what was accepted and respected in "the world", "society", "culture", and even the value system of my own parents' family.

I have the same feeling about this book. I don't have a complete, coherent understanding with my rational mind. But, I'm satisfied to follow the prompting, or feeling that maybe I should do this because it's a persistent idea that has "come down" into my body/mind/spirit and it might even be guidance of Spirit, so I am choosing to surrender to this.

Another way to explain this that is a bit more oblique, but more honest, is that I don't even know "who" is writing this. Is it me? Am I writing, or is there some larger force or entity writing through me? Am I writing only about my own particular experiences and what they've meant to me? Or am I writing about a metaphor of the general principle of life, experience, and search for meaning, growth, and truth? It feels more like the latter… "I" am following this inner prompting because I feel I must and it's about more than just "me". In fact, that is one of the central messages and lessons of all these experiences – that, as Joseph Rael says, "We don't really exist" – at least not exclusively as a linear, limited, coherent narrative, or self-image, but "I" exist also, and perhaps more comprehensively, as a boundless, formless, unconditionally free, and open awareness. That open awareness is a fundamentally important aspect of who "I" am, and who we all are.

So, I feel I should share these weird, non-ordinary experiences just in case it gives some reader out there permission to notice, accept, and express similar intuitive experiences of non-ordinary reality in their own life. If that someone is you, that's awesome!

We don't have to see these experiences as strange, something to be ignored, or buried. Instead, we can see these experiences as having a guiding, balancing, integrating influence and capacity. I now see these experiences that way in my own life and I hope you will see parallels in your life too.

I believe we all have amazing experiences that are "no coincidence" and if we look at them, reflect, and work with them, they can give us insight, give our lives deeper meaning, make us happier, improve our conduct, and expand our awareness. I believe this is all part of a process that helps us remember the fullness of who we are. If this book reaches even one person in this way, it will be a success. I hope you enjoy it!

Michael Pedroncelli
Los Ranchos, New Mexico, USA
November 2018 to March 2019

Section 1 – Initiation

This section includes two powerful and profound experiences that changed the lives of my wife, Marie, and I. I call them Initiation because I now see them as important examples of Spirit calling me and showing me the path back to my true self through connection with others.

The first experience was a 20 minute encounter with a beautiful soul on a bridge where she told us and showed us we were angels for her. She was an angel for us too, and by association and extension, we learned that we're all angels for each other.

The second experience is about a recurring vision and subsequent construction of a sacred space that led to a connection with a wonderful Native American medicine man named Joseph Rael (also known as Beautiful Painted Arrow), his teachings, and our experiences and connections with his beautiful extended community.

These are just two examples. There are many, many more such stories I could tell, and I may tell more in the future, but these are meaningful examples of how we receive what we need even if what we need sometimes comes in forms that are unexpected, unexplainable, or even unwanted.

Angels on the Bridge

On Monday, September 19th, 2011, the first day of a vacation trip to Taos Pueblo, Mesa Verde, and Chaco Canyon, my wonderful wife, Marie, and I had a life changing experience. We went to Taos first, with a stop along the way at the Santuario de Chimayo. Surprisingly, to us, we spent several hours at the Santuario chapel kneeling and praying with a few parishioners and the 92 year old pastor, Father Casimiro Roca. We prayed a rosary and stayed for a mass with them. Then, we got some sacred dirt in the miracle room on the side of the church.

We were feeling blessed and enjoying the beautiful weather and day except Marie was feeling sick. She said she felt like all her bones were broken. I kept asking her if she wanted to go back home. She said she thought she'd feel better and she insisted we continue.

We made it to Taos in the afternoon, found a B&B, and decided to go for a drive to the gorge bridge at sunset.

As we got to the center viewing platform, we noticed a lady across the bridge from us. I didn't pay too much attention to her at first. I was taking photos of the clouds and gorge.

The lady on the platform across the bridge asked if we had a cell phone. I told her, "No. Sorry. We don't." Marie said, "We usually do, but we left our cell phones at home since we're on vacation. We thought we might be better off without them this time. Hahaha... Sorry about that."

After we finished taking pictures, we headed toward the other side. As we approached, I paid closer attention to the lady. She was well dressed, clean, wearing designer sunglasses, hair kind of windblown and face slightly sunburned – probably 40 to 50 years old. She looked real fit and stylish - well put together but like she had spent a lot of time outdoors that day. I turned toward her, smiled slightly and nodded my head in a gesture of Namaste - "the God in me acknowledges the God in you". She seemed to return the acknowledgement and smile back. At that point I "felt" the aura of agitation around her, like she was an animal pacing a cage on that little viewing platform. It was like she "owned" that space so we didn't go there with her, but we went to the railing 10 or 15 feet away instead.

I looked at the view and took a few more pictures. As we finished taking the pictures and turned to walk back to the parking lot she said,

"Can I ask you a favor?"

I turned to look at her and from her body language I sensed that she was going to ask for something that was kind of like a con – tricking us into something we would later regret. I didn't want to say "No." because I thought that would be rude, but I didn't really want to say "Yes" either without hearing what it was first, so I said bluntly,

"What?"

She gestured to a man who was maybe 30 or 40 feet away and said,

"Can you keep that man away from me? He's creeping me out."

I told her "Yeah! We'll make sure you're safe and we won't let him harm you. But," I asked "what's going on? Has he done something to make you feel uncomfortable? Is he following you or something? Do you know him?"

"No", she said, "He's just kind of creepin' me out."

As we were speaking she was slowly raising her right knee on top of the platform railing and Marie leaned over and whispered (emphatically),

"She's climbing over the railing! She wants to jump!"

I didn't believe it because she was so calm, polite, well-spoken, and well dressed. I thought she was just stretching her leg or something. I wanted to keep her talking, move her off the bridge, and get her to feel safe about the guy who was "creeping her out" so I asked if we could walk her to her vehicle so she could be safely away from the creepy guy. She said "No. I've been having car trouble. It won't start." Her knee and ankle were up on the rail and she was kind of leaning forward holding on to the rail with both hands.

I asked "Are you OK?" She said, "Yeah, I'm OK."

I asked if we could drive her into town for a mechanic or wait with her at her vehicle until a mechanic came or something since the vehicle was giving her problems. She said she had AAA for that. I asked if she had called AAA and she said "Yeah." At that point I turned away from her and thought the best course of action was to walk away. I thought "I don't want to wait here with this lady who is creeped out by people for no clear reason, but yet refuses our reasonable offer to get away to safety. Apparently she wants to stay on the bridge for a while, and I don't want to just stand there with her. Maybe we're enabling her behavior by staying here and maybe she'll follow us if we just walk away." I still didn't think she was going over. I thought she was just a little strange. All those thoughts passed by in a split second. So, I turned my back and started to walk away.

Marie, in the meantime hadn't taken her eyes off her and had no intention of leaving since she was continuing to move over the rail. The lady then said something like,

"Well at least it's a beautiful place to wait."

There was something in her tone that was sweet and friendly and for lack of a better word - normal, so I turned back and said,

"Yeah, it IS beautiful here."

When I turned around she had one leg completely over the rail. She was straddling the top rail and holding on with both hands.

I told her firmly, "Please don't do that! Now you're creeping me out! That's not safe. Put your leg back on this side. You could fall off!" At that instant I knew Marie was right and she did want to climb over.

My mind panicked and I thought again "Turn and walk away and she'll follow. She'll only continue if she gets attention." But then in a split second I thought about whether I'd feel better about walking away from it or staying there and trying to talk her out of it if she actually did end up jumping. Again, in a fraction of a second, the instinct was to stay and talk with her. I felt certain that if I walked away, and she jumped I'd beat myself up more than if I stayed and did my best to keep her from jumping but she jumped anyway. And I thought, hey, maybe we can help her get through this impulse and talk her out of it and get her to walk back onto the bridge and away from the edge.

At that point Marie and I went into crisis intervention mode. As she straddled the rail, she looked over the edge longingly and lovingly, with only a slight hint of apprehension. She told us she was sorry but could we please make sure to call the number of the person she had written on a page that was on the dashboard of her blue Jeep in the parking lot. She said to have that person notify her husband. A thousand thoughts raced through my mind but I just tried to breathe, stay as calm as possible, and keep her talking. As she was talking, she was moving slowly but steadily over the railing, shifting her weight to the foot on the outside ledge of the platform, holding on to the rail very tightly with both hands, and moving her second leg outside of the bridge. Marie and I were watching her intently, but still talking calmly.

I thought about rushing toward her to physically pull her back in. But what if I stumbled and accidentally pushed her or what if I fell over the edge or what if rushing spooked her and made her jump right then? A thousand what if's in one second. "No", the calm, still voice from within answered. Better to talk calmly since she seems to be responding to that and try moving slowly toward her in a more controlled manner. So that's what we did. We kept talking and started moving slowly toward her.

I put my camera down.

She said "Don't get any closer and please don't take my picture."

I said "I'm not taking your picture and I won't do anything you don't want. I'm just putting the camera down because it's heavy."

That calmed her down. But I was panicked and was thinking about continuing to move toward her and grab her or get her in a bear hug and pull her back over or something like that. I was probably 5 or 6 feet away from the viewing platform and 10 or 12 feet away from her. Marie was closer to the platform but out in the road and a little bit closer to her than I was.

Marie asked if she could put her camera down and sit because her arm hurt from carrying the camera and her legs were hurting. The lady said "Yeah". At that point Marie sat on the curb in front of her maybe 8 feet away and I was to the side about 10 or 12 feet away. That's as close as she would let us get.

Marie asked if she could move to the "other side of the platform" [opposite side from me] so she wouldn't have to shade her eyes and look straight into the sun at her. She said "No. Stay right there."

I tried to step closer and she said, "Don't come any closer. Stay right there." I tried moving toward her a fraction of an inch at a time but steadily forward very slowly and as I did she started moving from leaning over the rail toward the bridge and tightly clasping both hands on the safe side toward standing up and loosening her grip.

She was like a frightened, wild animal that wouldn't let us get any closer than she was comfortable with. The choreography of the dance was such that she was clearly indicating she meant it. She was moving purposefully, but steadily and she intentionally reacted to any moves she didn't want by going faster and further over the edge.

I stood still at her side and Marie sat still at her feet. We suggested several times, gently but firmly, for her to just come back over and sit with us for a while. Here's an example of the kinds of things we were talking about:

Mike: "Let's go have dinner. We can find a good place to eat back in town and spend the evening together. We can stay up all night talking if you want. Then, we can figure out something good to do after that."

Marie: "Yeah. Or just come sit with us here on the curb. We'll be together as long as you want. We're on vacation so we can be together all week if you want and we'll talk for as long as you want."

Mike: "We'll be your friends forever, we'll never abandon you."

Marie: "It's true. He doesn't lie so if he says he'll do it he really will. Hahaha"

Lady on the Bridge: "I believe it. Hahaha."

We were hungry and perfectly OK with the thought of laughing, crying on each other's shoulders, hugging, and figuring out where to go next after a good meal and some rest back in town. We thought that she would feel the same way and those sentiments would be enough to bring her back over. Boy, were we wrong about that.

Lady: "Oh Bless You! But, NO! Please just call the number written down on the piece of paper on the dashboard of the blue Jeep in the parking lot."

We said we would.

The Lady said: "I'm sorry you have to be here for this and I'm sorry you have to see this."

We asked her what was going on in her life. What was she going through?

She said "There's just a lot going on right now."

We asked if she was going through stressful situations: was she going through any relationship, work, money, or health problems?

I told her, "Whatever it is, we can talk it out and figure out how to get through it together. We can build a support system and work through these temporary problems. They'll pass. These problems are temporary. You'll feel differently in an hour, a day, a week, a year. Things will get better. Let's talk about it."

We jabbered on to keep her there just a little bit longer.

She patiently and politely responded to all our questions, concerns, and comments. She said multiple times: "Bless You! I'm sorry you have to be here for this and I'm sorry you have to see this." But she just looked at us with a hauntingly knowing, patient, kindly gaze as if to say with her eyes and face, "You're kind and you mean well, but your words and sentiments are simplistic and off the mark. I know the truth, but I'll kindly humor you a bit more."

At one point she said: "*You two* were sent here for a reason. You're my angels."

She said: "My sister's dying of cancer, and ... there's just a lot going on right now."

We talked about her sister and their relationship. She said her sister's situation was dire and her household and relationships were in shambles and she had been going to visit her and help her clear things up as she approached her immanent death, but she couldn't do it anymore and she wouldn't go back again even though she felt she should. We said, it sounds like you've done plenty and there are surely others who can help her so you can take care of yourself right now. She nodded and said "Yeah".

    Me: "What else is going on?"

    Lady: "Mmmm, there's just a lot going on right now."

    Marie and I: "Do you have any kids?"

    Lady: " No."

    Marie: "Do you have any family?"

    Lady: "Not much, just my sister."

    Marie: "Stay here for your sister. She needs you!"

    Lady: "She'll be fine."

    Marie: "Be MY sister! Stick around for ME! I need you."

    Lady (smiling): "You don't have any sisters?"

    Marie: "I do, but they're mean to me. One of them tried to kill me. She pushed me off a horse."

    Lady: Smiles at Marie. Looks around. Tests the feel of being where she is. Springs up and down on her toes. Looks like she's going to jump at any moment.

    Mike: "What about your husband? Is he part of the problem? We could make sure you're safe from him."

    Lady: "No, no, NO! He's a wonderful man! The best husband a woman could have."

    Mike: "Well, if he's wonderful and your sister's dying, hold on for them. She needs you and he will help you through this. If he's truly a good man this will be the greatest blessing and gift of his life to be with you through this."

    Marie: "Yeah, let him be your strength – a shoulder you can lean on."

Lady: "Ummmm... No! They'll be fine." [With serious, calm, compassionate gaze and tone - not flippant or harsh at all.]

An odd thing that made all this surreal was that she was grinning a Mona Lisa smile the whole time, serenely calm in her body, enjoying the scenery around the horizon, looking down into the gorge, looking over toward us appreciatively with an open, friendly air as she tested the feel of the platform, checking to see if it felt like the right moment to jump RIGHT THEN. It was kind of like she was standing on her tiptoes with her back to the water on the edge of a high dive platform before diving backward into a local swimming pool for the first time. She was a little anxious but seemed more relaxed than anything and somewhat excited with it. There was also a sense of "I want and need to get over my fear, and do this." It seemed like she was either medicated with some anti-anxiety drug, extremely at peace with her decision and the situation, or both.

She was completely on the gorge side of the platform now, holding on to the top of the rail with both hands and leaning back.

As she would look around and away from us, Marie would gesture with her arms at passing vehicles, trying to get their attention so they would stop and help. People looked over and saw her hanging off the edge, but they just averted their gaze, shrugged their shoulders, and kept driving. Huh! What's up with these people!

Mike (to Lady): "Well if you don't want to lean on him [her husband] for your [Lady's] sake, do it for him."

Lady: "He'll be fine."

Extremely awkward silence!!! Hmmm. What to do? What to say?

Mike to Lady: "This is a permanent solution to a temporary problem."

Lady looks at Mike with very calm, wise, knowing, almost patronizing gaze and says, in an annoyed tone, "No, no, NO! I'm a psychiatric nurse!"

[Implying "You're not doing what I want my angels to do right now! You can't tell me anything I haven't told myself and others hundreds of times before. This line of reasoning and manipulation is not what I want or need right now. Please don't continue along these lines with worn out clichés designed for psychological and emotional manipulation."]

At this point I felt as though she was showing us through her words and actions, how we should be with her right then, and the answer was to be completely present, open, honest, peaceful, and loving. It actually felt like she was counseling US and waiting until we were ready for her to do what she was going to do.

Mike: "You're a nurse? Where do you work?"

Lady: "I've worked all over but mostly in Santa Fe."

Mike: "Do you live in Santa Fe?"

Lady: "No. We live near Santa Fe, in Glorieta. But I've done a lot of work in Santa Fe."

More awkward silence, confused, anxious thinking, praying, asking the universe for guidance, and looking for cues from her.

Then I made a big mistake. I thought one thing we hadn't tried was being her best friends - completely on her side against the rest of the world. Also we hadn't tried guilt. We tried a little friendship with the offer to go into town for dinner, and talking beyond this evening, and we tried a little guilt with "Stick around for your husband and sister." but not hardcore guilt and deep partnership. This all happened in an instant, and was just gut instinct (like everything else up to now).

Mike: "Well if you want to hurt your husband, there are better ways to do it than this, hahaha."

At that point, she moved her hands from the top rail over to the vertical rails on the gorge side. She slid her hands way down with her feet firmly planted and her butt sticking way out, bending her knees and bouncing her legs looking like she was going to do a big backward swan dive right then.

Mike (screaming): "No, no, no! I'm sorry! I didn't mean to say anything wrong! I didn't mean to be disrespectful to you. I won't do anything you don't want me to! Tell me what you want."

Mike (calming down, trying to calm her down and keep her hanging on for just one more minute at a time): "You said we're you're angels. Help us be your angels. What should we do? I know there's a positive intent behind what you're trying to do. Help us understand the positive intent and bring it to whatever it's supposed to be."

She slides back up, appears calm, thinks for a moment, then looks toward us and says thoughtfully: "Just BE with me."

Mike and Marie: "OK. We're good at that. We can do that!"

We spent about 30 seconds or a minute or two of silent stillness together feeling empty and at peace. We looked at the pastel sunset colors in the sky and clouds, felt perfectly comfortable with the fading light, warm air, and gentle breeze. It was kind of like meditation with eyes wide open or a lucid dreaming state.

Lady: Looking at us. Smiling. Looking around. Eyes blinking. Going inward and outward. Calm. Then, she starts springing on her toes again, testing the loosening of her grip, looking down. Testing the feeling. Seems like she's going to let go of her hands and "accidentally" lose her balance right then and there.

Mike: "What else?"

She (thinks again for a few seconds before responding – looks over at us very intently): "Never forget me. My name's Pam Barich. It sounds like parish but is spelled B-A-R-I-C-H. I'm a nurse in Santa Fe."

Mike and Marie: "Of course we'll never forget you. How could we? We're going to spend years together starting with dinner in town tonight. Come on with us, come back over to this side. Don't do this." Yada, yada, yada.

The more we talk, the more she loses interest and tests the jumping posture. It seems like she's getting tired of holding on. Almost seems like drugs are kicking in stronger, or she's just weary of life, really at the end of it all with no more strength to hold on or continue – or some combination of both.

Mike, almost in tears: "Pam, you're breaking my heart right now."

Pam, calmly: "I'm sorry."

Mike: "What else can we do? As your angels, what are we supposed to do right now? We're pretty new at this angel thing."

Pam (smiling, thoughtfully): "Are you religious? Catholic?"

Marie: "I'm supposed to be Catholic but I don't go to church any more. I made up my own religion."

Pam and Marie exchange knowing glances. They smile and giggle.

Pam: "Haha. I know what you mean. Me too!"

Mike: Smiles. "Me too."

...pause...

Pam: "I knew you were good people when I saw you. That's why I asked you to come over here."

Long pause. She gets serious, looks at us with the utmost seriousness and says: "Pray for me."

Afterward, Marie said she had been praying all along. But, I finally started praying as well immediately at that moment for her and with her, sending heartstrings, loving arms from our hearts, positive feelings, light, love, energy, calling the great spirit, holy spirit, spirit guides, angels, God, saints. We held her with our eyes and our hearts, and she was completely supported and safe, forgiven, free of all sin, and loved. She felt it and reciprocated with the utmost pure, deep, sincere look of gratitude and appreciation. It was a moment of poignant beauty, and a divine state of grace. It felt as if she jumped then, she would float in midair and be magically transported back onto the bridge safe and sound.

And yet, I knew that would not happen. I knew if she let go she would fall into the gorge, her body would be shattered, and her life would end. I didn't know what would happen with her soul, but I was more concerned with her soul than her body. The veil between the physical and spirit world was very thin. She was fully present, conscious, and aware. Her human body, mind, and her "soul", were communicating with us, but we had a strong feeling it would come to an end any instant now. She was VERY alive and so were we. We were all three in a state of love, sorrow, and surrender to the maximum degree. We all knew she would jump and there was nothing we could do but be with her, bless her, and not judge her for what she was doing because that's what angels do for each other. We were her angels and she was our angel.

After a few seconds or a couple of minutes of that (who knows, time stood still) it looked like she was really ready now. She was going to let go.

Marie started pleading with her: "No! Don't do it! Please. Don't do it. Stay here for me. Come sit with me and I promise no one will bother you. Don't do it! No!"

Marie: "How about if you wait until we call that phone number you want so you know we've called it? Will you wait for that?"

Pam: Crouched into a jumping position.

Marie: "I'll go get the number and call right now, just promise you won't jump."

Marie turns and starts moving away to go get the number.

Mike: "Let me go instead. You guys are getting along better anyway so it would be better if I went."

Pam stands up.

Marie and Pam look at each other, smiling and nodding.

Pam: "Yeah it WOULD be better if you go."

[Big smiles...]

"OK. I'll wait until you call the number."

Mike: "I'll get it as fast as I can."

I didn't want to abandon Marie but Marie and her seemed to be on the same wavelength, I thought it would be OK. Plus I needed a break. I was afraid I would say something that would cause her to jump, like I almost had before, so I went to get the number from the blue Jeep.

It seemed like it took forever. I wanted to run but thought I was going to pass out or throw up or something, so I took some deep breaths, slowed down and walked quickly. I went and got the number and returned as fast as I could. I saw signs in the Jeep that she had prepared to commit suicide (an apparent suicide note, an opened, nearly empty prescription bottle, her keys, driver's license and wallet on the driver's seat, and other clues). But, I also thought I saw signs that maybe she wasn't sure if she wanted to go through with it (the driver's window was open enough for her arm to reach in, and she had blankets and pillows there, leading me to think maybe she'd decide to sleep in the vehicle or under the stars instead...)

I got back to the middle of the bridge as soon as I could. Some guys on motorcycles had stopped and they called the number from the Jeep. We let Pam know we had called. At that point she had climbed farther over the edge only her fingers were visible holding on to the bottom of the railing.

Police cars arrived. Officers got out and blocked traffic. One officer got out and started moving steadily toward her. I don't know if he even saw her fingers there. Marie was sitting or standing just a few feet in front of her crying and saying "No, PLEASE don't do this." The officer walked steadily forward and Marie yelled at him to stay back saying that she didn't want people close.

The officer moved to the edge, and Pam let her feet hang from the platform, and let out a big sighing breath. We could only see her fingertips hanging on supporting all her weight. They started to get white and after about 3 to 5 seconds, the fingers slipped free.

I felt guided by something outside of myself not to go to the edge and look over. I felt I had to forcefully walk away to protect myself. I didn't want to see her hit and I knew I would have felt strongly pulled over. So I turned and walked away. Another officer was walking toward me. He asked "What's going on?" I yelled at him "IT'S DONE. SHE'S DEAD!"

It takes about 6 seconds for objects in free fall to get from the top of the bridge to the bottom of the gorge. There was perfect silence, then a loud SLAP(!!!) sound that echoed through the canyon.

I turned to look for Marie and when she wasn't right by my side walking away, I felt again as if controlled by some outside force and yelled "IT'S DONE. STEP AWAY FROM THE RAIL AND DON'T LOOK OVER THE EDGE!"

Marie had instinctively – as if in a trance, she said - gone up to the railing and leaned over. She felt her arm extending all the way to the water underneath Pam as if it was a long shadow. Marie saw her just before she hit the water. She fell with her back to the water and face up to the sky.

Marie says when I yelled it snapped her out of her trance and she stepped away and started following me.

Two of our different spiritual friends told us independently of each other that her soul left her body before she hit the water and Marie's shadow hand helped prevent her soul from being shattered so that her soul could remain intact.

We embraced and started crying. I was sobbing uncontrollably and said something like "I should have grabbed her hands or got her before she climbed over." Then a quiet strength washed over me in a second as if a wave of some external energy was guiding me. I stopped crying and said "It's not our fault. There's nothing more we could have done. It was her choice and we have to respect it." The main Officer was there with us as were the men on motorcycles who had made the calls from their cell phone. We all nodded in grave agreement that there was nothing more we could have done. They all told Marie and I it wasn't our fault, don't blame ourselves, we did our best and our best was VERY good.

I stayed on the bridge and talked with the policemen about what happened and gave them our contact information. Marie went back to our truck in the parking lot at the end of the bridge and she started talking to a lady from an adjacent vehicle.

When I finished talking on the bridge and joined them in the parking lot, I started admonishing Marie in a kind of harsh tone, "Why did you go up to the rail and look over? You could have fallen! Did you think you were supposed to rush over there or something?" Marie and the stranger looked at me with eyes that said "Why are you yelling at her?" I lowered my eyes and head and said I was sorry, that I was in a swirl of emotions and I was mad at something but I didn't know what and I knew it was wrong to be taking it out on Marie.

Some guy in traffic was talking real loud to other people in traffic saying he didn't know why they had traffic stopped because she was already dead anyway. Marie got mad, stormed over to him and yelled "What's wrong with you. Someone just died. Don't you have any respect you @#%@#$@!"

The lady I was with who had been talking with Marie at our truck was surprised Marie was going off and she was about to go help Marie, but I told her "No, she needs to let out some emotion too, like I just did with her. Too bad for that guy it had to be him." We both smiled. The guy didn't say anything. He turned around and drove off back toward Taos. A few other people who were around her said, "You're right", "Are you OK?", "It'll be OK..."

Marie came back and introduced me to the lady. Marie said the lady was pulling out of the parking lot but saw Marie had her head in her hands and saw that Marie looked distraught, so she got out of her vehicle and asked if Marie needed anything. Marie said "A hug". The lady asked me if I needed a hug too. I started crying again and said I did. Why didn't I think of that? Yeah. A hug! That's what I needed right then. So all three of us hugged and cried. We told her a short version of what happened, and we realized, and we told that lady she was OUR angel. She told us we were very brave and kind and that not many people would have handled it that well and been able to help her feel she was not judged and honor her. It was very beautiful what that lady said.

Just then, the main officer, Sgt. X, drove up and said he still needed information – he forgot to get our address or phone number or something. He asked if we were OK and said he could help us get connected to someone to talk to if we needed. We said, "Thanks but we think we're OK." He advised us to be very careful driving back into town and wherever we were going. He said we "probably wouldn't sleep tonight." And he advised that we "probably shouldn't try to drive all the way back to Albuquerque tonight."

Marie started telling Sgt. X about our plans for a weeklong vacation, going to Taos Pueblo tomorrow, then Mesa Verde and Chaco to tour Native ruins and sacred sites and also our plan to visit a Native medicine man, Joseph Rael, in Colorado. Marie said, we'll rest in town tonight and see how we feel tomorrow, but we really want to go on this trip. I said, I thought it would be better for us to continue with the trip instead of going back home and stewing in the aftereffects and our feelings and involvement around this event. Sgt. X said he was from Taos Pueblo, that it's a beautiful place and there's lots of peace there. He said it would be good for us to go there tomorrow. He opened up his heart and spoke to us in a way that healed us very deeply. Sgt. X told us a little about his spiritual beliefs and how he had learned to cope with these losses of life on the bridge over the 18 years he had worked there. His testimony was beautiful and very healing to us. One of the things he said was something like "One thing I've learned is that all the people who do this have already made up their mind. They've made peace with their God, or Allah, or Buddha, or whatever they believe and there's nothing you can do to stop it. ... If you have any kind of religious beliefs, just pray." We thanked him for his deep goodness and decency and the healing influence of his words. We shed more tears and expressed additional gratitude. He told us again we could receive follow up grief counseling for free if we chose and reminded us to be careful. He was another angel to us.

Then, as we drove off in the dark toward Taos for the night, we started "never forgetting" and we "just prayed".

~~~~~~~~~~~~~~~

Even though it seems like this would be a difficult, or even traumatic, experience, we felt blessed by it. She said we were her angels, and we knew and felt deeply that was true. But, she was our angel too. She was so patient, kind, gentle, and completely open-hearted and present, that she taught us something profound.

And Sgt. X's comment about everyone having their path and destiny and making up their own mind felt right too. Then, even the other people we met, were all angels to us. Even the hugging lady in the parking lot.

A week later we met her husband, Dr. Willard (Bill) Dean. We learned he was an amazingly kind and wonderful man and we became close friends. He has been another angel for us as we have for him.

This astounding experience changed our lives. After this we learned we're all Angels for each other. We knew Pam had to do this. We knew she was at peace with the decision and God and the Spirit World. We also realized this was "right" and "good" for her. It was an act of kindness and forgiveness and release for herself even though it defied cultural norms of morality or decency. And we would not have received these messages and lessons and met Pam and Bill and had this amazingly deep and open connection with them and such an intimate connection with life and death if we had gone in a different direction, or at a different time. Clearly, this was so powerful and important for us, it was "meant to be".

Joseph Rael and the Circle of Light Peace Chamber

Another profound, non-ordinary experience has been ongoing for over 30 years. This, more than anything else, has moved me toward "remembering who I am" and has shown me that much of who I am and who we all are cannot be "explained" or "understood" with the judging, categorizing, "rational" mind. This realm of phenomena is called non-ordinary consciousness, non-ordinary reality, mystic, psychic, visionary, or miraculous. When one experiences this kind of "super-consciousness", that involves connection beyond any sort of physical explanation, one begins to *know* that we really are limitless, and anything *really is* possible.

~~~~~~~~~~~~~~~~~~

It started sometime in the 1980's. I began seeing a building in my Mind's Eye. It was cylindrical in shape with an opening in the middle of the roof like a Native American kiva, but different from a kiva in that it had a door on one side. And also, it was different than most kivas in that it was half underground and half above ground. I didn't have many recurring dreams at that point in my life - in my early 20's. But, this dream kept coming back. Sometimes, I'd have the dream at night. Other times, it would pop into my head during the daytime. When I saw this structure, it always seemed bright and "full of light". It was made out of adobe (dried mud bricks), and it had no windows. I had the impression I was supposed to build this structure wherever I could, probably near my home. The dream and vision was so persistent, it kept coming back over a period of years and eventually the years stretched into decades. I have not had any other dream that continued like that, so persistently, and so clearly, for such a long time.

In our 20's, 30's, and early 40's, my wonderful wife, Marie, and I were busy living life, working full-time, raising our three sons, and even welcoming another generation as our oldest son, Rob, had kids and got married. My job, our kids, and our household were our priority. So I didn't get around to building this structure for over 25 years. But as I approached age 50, our kids moved out of the house. They were establishing their independence and doing well. And, I began to see a possibility and feel strongly that I should retire from my career as an electronic technician, then software engineer, group leader, and project leader at a government research and development organization and switch to a financially modest, but more free, open, and spiritual way of life at age 50 or as soon thereafter as possible. As I approached that life transition, thoughts of the kiva started coming forward again.

In 2009, I attended a New Mexico Men's Wellness Spring Retreat where we drew timelines of our lives on a big sheet of paper that stretched across a wall. The idea was to see if we had common patterns in the ups and downs and loop-de-loops of our lives across the decades. When my friend Doug got up to talk about his timeline, he said the 80's were one of the best times in his life because he and his wife spent a lot of time with a Native American medicine man named Joseph Rael.

As soon as Doug said the name Joseph Rael, I went into something like a waking dream state. I was floating above and slightly behind the left shoulder of a small Native American Man as he walked through a high desert canyon. He had a brightly

 colored cloth on his head for a headband. He had fine features and wonderful energy. He was walking with such vitality and vigor – neither in a hurry nor slowly, but deliberately, with great concentration, awareness, clarity, and purposefulness. As he walked past the dirt, rocks, and desert plants, they all vibrated with light, color, and sound. Each had its own unique type of resonance and vibration. I couldn't tell if he caused the vibration as he moved past, or I was sensing his awareness of the vibration that was already there, inherent in the objects. Either way, however it worked, the vibration was more apparent as he walked by. Things came alive in a wave near him as he passed by, and there was a resting, joyful, rejuvenated vibration along his path after he went by. He clearly possessed an extraordinary awareness and/or ability to activate vibration. I could sense his temperament, his thoughts, his joy, and feel the lightness of his being. He seemed to be chanting silently in his mind and performing ceremony as he walked. He was a beautiful Man – physically, emotionally, and spiritually. I paid attention to the vibration of his thoughts, his movement, and his appearance as fully as I could so I could remember him.

Then, just as quickly as I entered the vision, I exited, and I was back in the meeting room hearing Doug complete his sentence about spending time with Joseph doing ceremonies in New Mexico and Colorado.

I didn't mention this to anyone at the conference weekend because I didn't want them to think I was strange, but I did make it a point to remember the name "Joseph Rael". When I got back home I Googled Joseph Rael. I learned he was also called Beautiful Painted Arrow and found lots of images and descriptions of his books, audio, video recordings, and artwork. The pictures looked like the Man I saw in the vision – especially the younger photos. The bright headband was the same. It was him! I saw him in this vision the very first time I heard his name. This really hit me with a strong force because I didn't have visions like this – EVER – at least not before that.

I browsed around the internet and found that two of Joseph's main insights, teachings, and works were about:

1.) Vibration. He said (and says) everything is made out of energy that is vibrating.
   [This matched the vibration of light, color, and sound that I saw in the vision of him when I heard his name.]
2.) Sound Peace Chambers. Joseph had visions to spread the word for people to build structures that he called Sound Peace Chambers. These were round or oval buildings. He envisioned them built around the world with ceremonies performed globally at the same time each month and throughout the year so they would link up energetically through the Earth to create Purification, Peace, and Harmony.

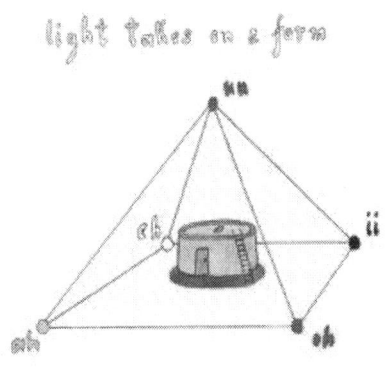

As I searched online, I saw pictures of Peace Chambers around the world that had been built by followers of Joseph Rael since the 80's. Picture after picture looked just like my visions of the building I was supposed to build.

I learned that Joseph had his Chamber vision in the summer of 1983, and he built the first one in 1984 where he was living in Bernalillo. This chamber was 10 to 15 miles from where I lived when I started having the visions in the 80's (and where I still live). I believe Joseph's vision and his chamber activated a vibration in me across that distance, at that time, back in in the 80's, and continuing on into the present. I feel this was some sort of soul-level message for me.

Joseph's first Sound Peace Chamber in Bernalillo, completed in 1984
(no longer in existence in physical form)

Once I learned about these chambers, I knew what I had been seeing all these years wasn't a kiva, it was a Sound Peace Chamber.

I realized I had three connections with Joseph and I felt it was profoundly important to pay attention to this in my life even though I could not understand it with my rational mind.

1. The first connection to Joseph was the recurring vision of the Peace Chamber I was supposed to build.

2. The second connection happened in 1987. A few days after our youngest son Carlos was born, we had to come up with a middle name for the birth certificate before we could take him home from the hospital. On the spot, out of the blue, I said, "His middle name is Rael". Several people said "What? That's not a middle name! That's a last name." But I felt it *was* the proper name for Carlos and we stuck with it.

3. The third connection to Joseph was this vision of him walking in ceremony in the high desert where he was activating and/or observing the vibration of all things around him.

Finally, with that third connection – the vision in 2009 - and the subsequent information from the internet, it all came together and I knew Joseph Rael and the Chamber were important for me. I felt an urge to meet Joseph and build the Chamber.

First Meeting with Joseph

Marie's Mom was critically ill and I was up to my eyeballs at my job in 2009 and early 2010, but after Marie's Mom passed away in May 2010, we had a chance to take our first vacation in years. We decided to go to Colorado to meet Joseph.

Leading up to that trip, in August 2010, I had nighttime dreams of going to Joseph's house and meeting him at his Chamber. In my dreams, I saw his house. It was yellow and nestled on the side of a small hill or bluff.

I read on one of the web pages that he lived on property near or on Southern Ute land. Based on the dreams and that bit of information, I truly believed all we had to do was get in the car, start driving, and Spirit would guide us straight to his door. We drove to Colorado to find him. As it turned out, we didn't find his place or connect with him in person on that trip. But we did manage to get the phone number of one of Joseph's daughters - Geraldine. I told her my story, and she said her Father was retired and he was no longer doing "that kind of work" but she'd let him know about us and let him decide if he wanted to contact us.

We hung around town for a couple days, then explored wilderness in Southern Colorado for the rest of the week. We didn't get a call while we were in Colorado. We were sad, but we knew it wasn't meant to be.

Instead, something even better happened. When we got back home to Albuquerque, we had a message on our answering machine saying "Hello, this is Joseph Rael and it would be fine if you come visit me. Here are the directions and here is my phone number." We were on cloud 9! We called and told him we were back in Albuquerque, but we could head to Colorado the following weekend. He said, "Well I'm going to Albuquerque on Monday. We can meet there." We offered to have him to our home for a meal so he could see the site where we planned to build a chamber. We were ecstatic waiting for him to arrive.

When I first met Joseph, he said "Hello Brother" and gave me a hug with the warmth of greeting a long-lost relative. With very little introductory small talk, he said we were brothers in a previous life, but in that life I was in angelic form! I was bowled over with his sweetness, generosity, and the matter-of-factness of his statement.

He invited me up to his Hotel room at the Sandia Casino and we talked for maybe 15 minutes. He asked me what was going on in my life and what a typical day was like for me. I was outwardly pretty calm, but inwardly nervous and excited like a person would get when meeting a rock star, or big celebrity they adored. I rattled on. I can't remember what I said. He acknowledged each thing I said calmly, showing that he understood. I had a sense he was reading me and he could see beyond the words and he "knew" more about me than I was telling him. At some point, I felt like he felt I was "OK". He stopped the small talk and asked if I would like to know the meaning of my name from a Tiwa-language sound perspective. I said yes. It was beautiful, but I can't remember much of it. I know it started with "manifesting awareness" (Mah - Ee). I melted into a state of bliss. I felt like I had died and gone to heaven. He asked if I was ready to go to our house to meet Marie and have dinner. I said yes. On the way out I noticed he had an email printed out sitting on top of his dresser. It was an email that I had sent to him through his publisher months earlier. In it, I described my three connections to him.

As we drove the 15 minutes or so from the casino to our house, we were quiet for several minutes. I could tell Joseph knew that I wanted to talk and ask questions, but he sat in silence with me. I enjoyed the silence with him, so I just stayed quiet. I felt we both loved this moment tremendously as brothers reunited.

After a while, I'm sure I jabbered something about the weather, or whatever. Joseph was polite and he responded. But, after the next pause, Joseph said "So, you have visions too, huh?" Up to this point, I felt he was the big, wise guru, and I was the learner. But, when he said that, I looked at him, and he had a relaxed, calm, confident, but kind of impish grin and I felt that he saw me as an equal – a true brother. I said "Well, I've had a few, but very few visions. The only visions I think I've had are the recurring vision of the chamber, the vision of you in the canyon with the vibration, and in dreams. Those are pretty much the only visions I've had." I looked at him and he nodded, but seemed to be asking, "Really? Say more..." with his body language and eyes. I said, "I think my rational mind is too dominant and whenever intuitive stuff comes in, the rational mind turns it away and I can't follow it." He just smiled and nodded and said "Yeah. That's how it works sometimes, huh."

After another pause, I told him I'd been interested in past lives and I had been having the feeling there was something important for me that I should know from past lives. He said "We usually don't get to experience that. We're not allowed to see it because it would keep us from living the life we're in now. It would be too distracting. Apparently, that's the way God designed it." He had a twinkle in his eye and a gentle smile, but I also felt there was a deep and profound seriousness about what he said and his manner in general. At that moment, I felt he conducted himself in word, movement, gesture, and posture as if his every thought and word and movement was creating the world. I was blown away with his gentle, quiet, calm humility, and yet, at the same time, subtle and profound power. I said, "Maybe that's why we don't get too many visions too – maybe they can be distractions from the importance of everyday life and relationships." He smiled and nodded yes. After another brief pause, he said "You know, we really don't exist." I'll never forget that moment. We were parked at a stoplight at 4th and Alameda in Albuquerque and I felt rushed to defend my existence with a verbal and intellectual argument. I said, "Well, we exist, but not in the way we normally think we do. I think we're more subtle, and expansive, and multi-dimensional than we can even imagine." He seemed to be a little disappointed in my response. Before, he was turned toward me and he had an inquisitive posture, but after I said that, he turned to sit looking straight forward and he just said, "Yeah." He didn't have the impish grin and we didn't continue the dialogue. I wondered why there was a shift in his posture, or if there was at all, and what should I say next. This was normal, self-conscious stuff, but for some reason, I felt that our mystical bro connection stopped at that point. Maybe I was too sensitive and just over-interpreting. But, afterward, for years, I thought about that, and I wondered what he meant by "We don't exist." It seemed like he wanted to tell me something or explore further, but my comment shut down the flow.

After this pause, I lapsed into a bit of hero worship. I told Joseph, "I've read some of your books and listened to some of your interviews, teachings, and lectures Joseph and I think you've tapped into divinity at the same level as the highest mystics – like Jesus, or Buddha." Without even the slightest hint of ego, pride, or false humility, Joseph replied, "Well, we Indians are pretty primitive. We are simple so we can hold the center." I asked if he meant simple relative to technology, and information, and material wealth. He nodded. Again, I was so blown away, I didn't know what to say. So, I just nodded and smiled and we drove the rest of the way in wonderful silence.

Joseph, my wife Marie, and I spent the afternoon together and had a wonderful "Pueblo" dinner at our house with rice, beans, squash, green chile, and fresh, homemade tortillas. He said thank you for the lovely meal but he shouldn't eat much. He said too much salt and sugar keep a person from having visionary experiences.

Marie showed Joseph some of her art. He liked it and when she went into the kitchen he told me "She has a nice vibration." Marie spontaneously gifted him one of her drawings. He showed us a picture album with Chamber photos. There were two loose Polaroids in there. He said, "These are photos of my Chamber. I want you to have them."

Pictures of Joseph's Chamber he gave to Mike and Marie during his visit to Albuquerque in 2010

The picture of the chamber looked just like the building I had seen in the dreams before the trip to Colorado.

We took Joseph to the site in our yard we were considering for our future Chamber and he went into an ecstatic, visionary kind of state. He had a big smile and said the spot made him "Feel that he wanted to go down into the Earth." He said it would be "fine, very fine" to build a Chamber there. Then, he said with a smile that if we felt we should move it from that spot, we could call him up and ask him if the new place would be OK, and he would say "yes, it's OK", or we could just move it without calling him. We did end up moving it. Somehow Joseph knew, even then, that we would move it. I remember he also said that when he asks the spirits why we're here and why we're doing this work, they tell him, "We're here to expand people's consciousness from here to HERE." As he said this, he was looking at Marie and I and he gestured with his palms close together in front of his body, then he moved his arms wide open, outstretched to the sides. He also said something about how reality has endless layers. He said reality is like a book. It has an overall story and energy, but when you open it up you get a lot from even each side of just one page. Then he paused and looked at us in the eye and said, "But you if you look inside that one page and open it up, inside the page is a whole other book." That was a bit of a head scratcher, but also an eye opener. I thought I understood what he was talking about...

We had an indelible 4 hours together. It was a real pleasure, privilege and honor to have that visit. Joseph said so many wise and wonderful things, and there was a real "transmission" and "expansion of consciousness" for Marie and I just being in his presence.

Construction of a Chamber in Albuquerque

We broke ground in July 2011. It got off to a slow start. I borrowed a Bobcat from a coworker and on the second day, I had an accident where I tipped over the Bobcat. Fuel and hydraulic fluid leaked out on the ground. I thought it was a disaster and the sacred Chamber was ruined and doomed.

I was saddened and depressed, and I thought it was a "bad omen". I was paralyzed for a few days. I didn't know what to do. But miraculously, as always, throughout the construction of this chamber, I received guidance about what I needed so that I could proceed. I heard a radio news discussion about a fuel contaminated site and how they cleaned it up. One of the panelists said, "It's not difficult to clear small spills. Small spills can be dug out and the dirt can be sampled along the way until there are no more traces of fuel. The contaminants are cleared out when the soil no longer has dark spots or foul smell." So, I did that. I got the Bobcat out of the hole, then, dug out the fuel contaminated soil by hand with a shovel. It didn't take long and it wasn't hard.

I saw this as a metaphor for what we humans are doing to the Earth as a species on a global scale and took it as a sign to simplify and slow down. Instead of trying to attack this project in haste, I was supposed to meet it gently, in a state of grace. I received a clear message - "Slow Down. Enjoy it. It's a Labor of Love. Enter into Deep, Sacred Time. This is not a place for Hurry, Stress, Striving, or Struggle." I received this message on the second day of construction, then, over and over through the construction, and I'm receiving it still.

Over the next year, I dug the rest by hand with a shovel on nights and weekends. My Men's group helped me one day and a friend helped for a couple hours on another day. The rest I dug myself. Digging this was definitely a spiritual practice and Labor of Love. The digging was complete to the point where further construction could proceed around July 2012, over 25 years after my first visions, a year after breaking ground, and a few weeks after I retired from my career of 29 years.

Guided by Spirit

Every step of the way, my conscious mind was trying to decide how to build this structure. But the conscious mind couldn't understand or decide. I was only able to receive intuitive guidance. It would first come in as "inspiration", then the conscious mind would evaluate. This was very unusual for me. I was usually a left brain, logical, rational, deciding, categorizing, planner first, then execute-the-plan type guy. But the way my mind and intuition worked with this chamber project was totally different. It was like the chamber itself was training and teaching me how to open up to intuition.

For example, I "thought" the structure was supposed to contain "all natural" materials. I thought it was supposed to have zero modern, man-made, heavily processed materials. My mind clung to this idea having been influenced by the Bobcat fiasco. Clinging to the idea held me back. I was also racked with indecision about everything. The logical mind kind of just "locked up". But, I noticed if I would get quiet and patiently wait for subtle intuitive feelings that felt like messages of spiritual guidance that came from outside of myself and moved through a different part of my mind and body than I usually paid attention to, it became easier to move forward, little by little. I was forced to meditate and get clear to be able to receive these type of messages and guidance.

At times I felt the presence of spirits around me there at the site, including other Chamber builders, ancient Anasazi kiva builders, and other kindred spirits including creators of sacred sites throughout all history and from all over the world and other worlds. The chamber itself had a spirit, energy, personality, and/or mind too.

Multiple times, I felt a whole crew of Anasazi guys crawling around. There were young guys who loved to laugh, joke, poke fun at me and make light of the project. They'd say things like "He doesn't know what he's doing. Look how funny this is. Hahaha." There were also some older, wiser, slightly more serious Anasazi guys in the crew too. If I had a question, I'd ask this choir of angels, "What do you think?", and they'd say "It'll be fine to do it that way. Here's another way that would be fine too…"

Over time, I let Spirit guide me more and more, especially the Anasazi crew and the Spirit of the building itself. I also noticed there was a kind of guardian angel-like spirit that was involved. This guardian angel provided encouragement, reassurance, and comfort to me personally and it seemed to be very interested in my relationship to this project, process, and structure. I found the guardian angel to be a very reassuringly calm, patient, loving, cheerful, strong, kind, and caring ally.

The Earth, the Sun, and the whole cosmos were also involved in the project and they communicated with me. The Earth told me all materials are natural – everything on this planet comes from the Earth and the Sun(!). The consciousness and intelligence of the building itself told me that it was an ancient, timeless structure. It was decaying even as it was being built, and that was part of its essence. It was an example of decay and birth, rising and falling, coming into being and disappearing, solidity and ephemerality. The guardian angel and the Anasazi's and other sacred site and sacred structure builders and lovers let me know "Everything was OK. Keep going."

For a long time, as I was building it, I wasn't sure what to do about the size of the building, the foundation, walls, specifics of the door, or the design and construction of the roof. But, the Spirits guided me and helped answer questions. Each step along was a journey of faith. The Spirits, Earth, and the building let me know a little bit of concrete, metal, and other modern materials would be OK. I felt their messages in the form of very subtle intuitive messages or "ideas" that felt very clear and correct – kind of like telepathic communication.

The Doorway

After the digging, I was ready to install the doorway. For the door posts, I played with different sizes and finally *felt* the opening was supposed to be 44 inches wide by 88 inches tall. I used an old viga (round wooden post) from around our yard that was left over from building our house. The door posts were set on concrete piers that extended two feet into the earth and stuck up about a foot above the ground. The spirits guided me on all this BIG time.

The doorway went in the last days of August and first days of September 2012. It was a big turning point. After that, there was a threshold into the sacred space. It gave a sense of roof height and how the space would feel once it was built. The whole space became much more real. Another threshold on the path had been created and crossed.

The Bench / Foundation for the Adobe Wall

Next, I had difficulty deciding what to do about the foundation of the walls. I asked Spirit and trusted in their guidance and I got the answer. I sensed Spirit drawing my attention to the fact that the sand was uniform and compacted, and it would make a nice bench all the way around the edge and be a good foundation upon which to build walls. Building the walls on top of the sand bench would be stable since this sand had been deposited and compacted over hundreds, thousands, or maybe even millions of years. Plus, if water ever flooded in, it would soak into the bench and floor and evaporate or percolate down into the ground before it ever got to the adobes in the wall (so I thought at that point). Also, it saved me a couple of feet of digging and wall building.

When it came time to actually build and decide, I asked the Anasazi Spirits about it. They were strong and clear counsel on this. They thought encouraged me to do it this way. They said that's what they did in Chaco and Mesa Verde. So, it was settled, and the walls were built upon the existing sand that was already in the hole but on top of a circular bench that extended all the way around the circle from one edge of the door to the other.

One last problem – the exposed sand edge had to be stabilized to keep it from crumbling and eroding over time. The solution for that was to wrap it in chicken wire and cover it with a thin layer of mortar made with sand from the excavation, cement, and lime. Here are some pictures:

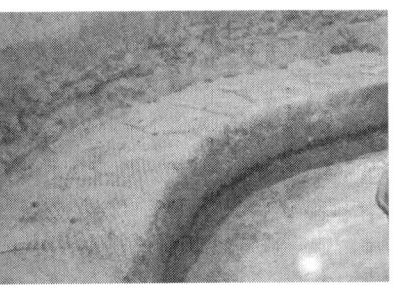

I want to point out three things here with these pictures:

1. First, Marie and I met as children and we used to play in the mud and make mud pies out of dirt from her yard and water from her hose. Marie had a few small pie tins and she'd make a batch of mud each morning to fill her mud pies. She'd put them in their horno (outdoor mud brick oven). By the evening, the mud pies would be "cooked". We're still having fun playing in the mud with each other 50 years later.
2. Second, I had a dream one night of this Chamber plastered with a sparkling mica clay. I thought "My God, how will I ever get that much micaceous clay and how can I possibly plaster the whole structure with it?" Well, as I dug down into the sand layer, I noticed it had thousands of little sparkles. Upon close inspection, I

found little quartz, or mica, crystals. So, the mica I needed was buried right there at the site!
3. Third, is in the upper left picture on the previous page. Note that there is a vein of different material near the bottom. As I was digging down, there was 9 to 18 inches of clay on the surface, then 3 to 4 feet of pure, sparkly, sand. I was disappointed that there was too much sand in the mixture to make good adobes. I thought I'd have to haul in more clay, but as I dug the last few inches, I came across another layer of clay. The clay layer was chock full of little white spiral shells. This told me that layer was a shallow sea or some kind of marsh, lake, river, or wetlands. From a metaphorical perspective, this meant that this site was linked to water, and the spirals meant it was linked to galaxies, and the universe. That was pretty cool! Also, the dirt with the shells was clay and the layer beneath had a mix of sand and clay. As it turned out, with those final layers, the dirt from the hole had the proper proportion of sand and clay to make good adobes.

The walls are made from sand and clay of the Earth that came from the space dug out from the top of the bench to the floor. This is another example of the miracle of receiving what is needed right from the heart of the middle of whatever we're doing, wherever we are. In this case it came from Earth beneath our feet at the bottom of the chamber.

Adobes / Wall

Two weeks after the doorway, on September 17, 2012, we laid the first adobes. I read books about adobes, thought, meditated, and planned this for a long time. I agonized over the decision to add a little bit of cement to the dirt to "semi-stabilize" the adobes and make them erosion resistant to rains and any water that might seep in over the months it would take to build the walls. I consulted the Spirits, but they were silent.

I didn't need to apply this much logical, rational brain function, or spiritual consultation to this. It was OK to rely on instinct, intuition, and the earlier guidance. A little cement was fine, so I added some to the adobes. I felt that the Spirits were intentionally silent and by being silent they were guiding and teaching me to trust myself.

For the next few months, up to early December 2012, Marie and I laid more adobes. First, we mixed the adobe mud in a wheelbarrow with a hoe, but that was HARD and slow! 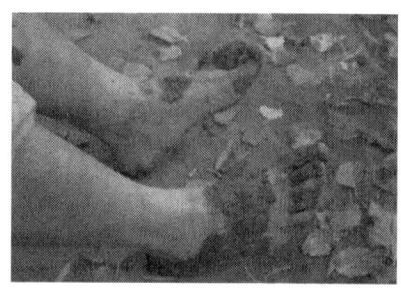 Next we spread out a tarp and made the adobes by mixing and stomping the dirt and water with our bare feet. We could do a few more adobes per day that way and it was fun to connect our bodies with the Earth like that, but the cement was hard on our skin. It was easier than mixing in the wheelbarrow with a hoe, but still HARD labor. When we were doing it that way, we'd work a day or two and rest two or three. Finally, when it got cold, we had only two or three hours late each afternoon where it was warm enough to stomp the mud without freezing our feet, so we switched to using a small electric mixer we borrowed from a friend. That mixer helped move things along a LOT quicker.

In early December, I started feeling an urgency to "finish" the Chamber by December 21, 2012, the great point in time demarcating the end of one cycle and the beginning of another on the Mayan Calendar. I was pushing hard and getting anxious again. I was in my own head, with my own thoughts. At that point, I had another lesson looming.

<u>Injury</u>

I got worn out, caught a cold and fever and couldn't sleep well for a couple of weeks. When I was finally starting to feel better, I passed out one afternoon for a nap and when I woke I couldn't move. I had excruciating pain in my lower back. I thought my back just "went out" like it had a few times before over the years. But this was more intense. I went to our chiropractor friend and rested. But, it was bad, REALLY bad, this time. It got a little better a couple of times but each time I pushed it and did too much activity or moved wrong, it went bad again or even worse. Through January and February it didn't get much better and I was in excruciating, debilitating pain. I could hardly do anything. I couldn't stand or walk or move much at all. Finally after about 12 weeks, I went to an orthopedic Doctor and got an MRI.

The MRI showed I had a ruptured disk in my lower back. This bulging disk was pressing on nerves that caused intense pain from the back down to my big toe where it felt like there was a big marble under the ball of my foot. It was a throbbing, burning, itching, tingling, numb ache that never went away. It was so intense, I couldn't think, plan, remember, or understand anything. I no longer had what I had known for the last 40(ish) years as my "mind". (I say 40 because the first 10 years as a child, I had a different mind – less conditioned, more awake, and pure.) I had to meditate, focus on breathing, and pay attention to the parts of my body that were OK, in spite of the constant, mind-numbing pain.

I went to a few healers. All of them helped me. Over a couple months, with physical activity, and learning how to move, and how not to move, I steadily improved. During this time I was scared and angry. I was mad it was taking so long and worried I might not get completely better. I gradually got better until I plateaued in a condition where I still had some pain and limitation. I considered cortisone shots or surgery. But instead, I decided to live with the limitation and see the whole process and remaining capacity of the body as a gift and miracle. I didn't know if I would be "all the way" better ever again. My future condition wasn't something I couldn't predict, or control. All I could learn to do was be aware of my condition from moment to moment. As I got better, little by little, I realized I was thankful for any capacity I had. I focused on all the health in my body and practiced being grateful for the capacity I still had instead of being sorry or bitter about what I had lost. I focused on the life principle and innate healing principles built into the dynamic intelligence of the cells and systems within the body itself. I gave thanks each day for the miraculous blessing of the body to heal and regenerate itself, the incredible mind, awareness and consciousness I was given, and the infinite expansiveness of Spirit.

I was actually in a state of spiritual ecstasy during that time. I spent several hours each day in meditation, prayer, and contemplation. I slept soundly all night and napped many days. My dreams were sweet and beautiful. During the day, the only tolerable positions for any extended period were lying down and sitting. Plus I could stretch, and walk a few minutes each day, with gradually increasing duration and intensity.

Marie took great care of me. I was in that condition for several months and it was a blast in its own way (maybe not for Marie though). Boy, this message to "slow down and enjoy" was even stronger than the previous one when the Bobcat tipped over, and this one was about as severe as it could get without stopping me entirely! What would it take for me to get the message?

Getting Started Again

In March, various friends said, "I want to help. Give me a date and I'll be there." But my friend and physician, Bill Dean (yes, Pam's husband), took it one step further and said, "How about if I come over on March 24th?" Bill came over and by a twist of fate, we had a young visitor at our house that same day who offered to help as well. Jeremy, the son of our friend Helene, got off the train from California, sat down at our table to share a snack, and joined Bill and I. Bill, Jeremy and Mike worked all afternoon. Jeremy loved it. That day got things moving forward again after almost 4 months of inactivity.

March 24th, 2013 with Bill and Jeremy

Inspiration

Shortly after that, on April 7th, 2013, we went with some friends, Jim and Mary, to see Joseph Rael at Ghost Ranch. We met some other friends there too, including Chittak, Herb, Doug, and Lyra (The same Doug who mentioned the name "Joseph Rael" that sent me into the vision in 2009). Joseph gave a beautiful talk, had an art show and book signing, and performed a fire ceremony.

Jim and Mary at Ghost Ranch before the talk.
Doug and Lyra with Joseph before the talk.

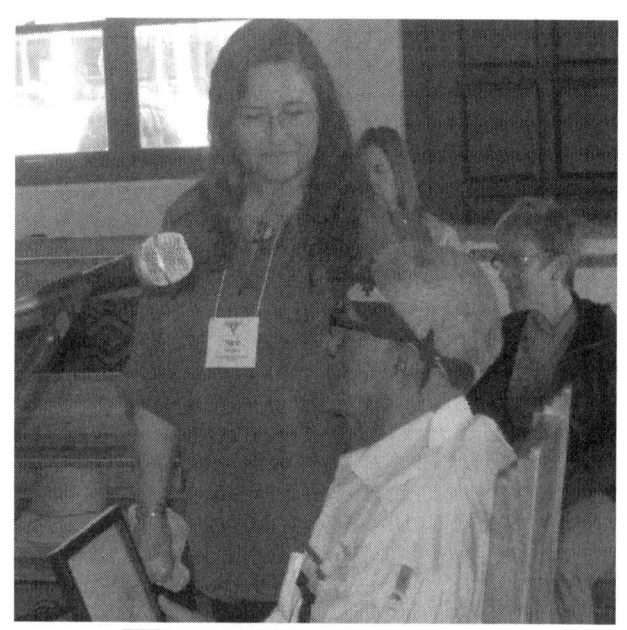

Marie and Joseph at the break in the middle of the talk.
Joseph and others at the fire ceremony.

At one point in the question and answer someone asked "Are there any Chambers in New Mexico and are they open to the public?" I blurted out, "Yeah, we're building one in our backyard and you can come." Joseph said "I've been there and I blessed it. But what you don't know (Mike and Marie), is that I was blessed by it too." A few people came over afterward and asked about it. That public announcement with Joseph was another impulse to keep working and get it built. Seeing Joseph was inspiring and wonderful. Afterward, Jim said "We need to get that Chamber built – before the monsoons!"

Completion of the Adobe Wall

Soon after seeing Joseph, Jim and Jeremy came over and provided lots of good energy, moving it forward. Jim and Jeremy loved working there so much, they came back several more times. Jim and Mike had several pleasant, productive days together. Jeremy and Mike bonded, talked about some big life choices, and got a lot done!

The guys from Mike's Men's group helped with adobes on the wall one day. Marie, Jeremy, Jim, and Mike made the rest of the adobes. The final adobe was completed on June 17th, 2013, nine months after the first adobe was laid.

It was such a joy working on and building this that it was bittersweet to complete it. But, everything moves along in its own time...

Feeling the Energy

At this point, the feeling in the Chamber was phenomenal. It was clean and clear, calm but powerful. Being in that space, gave a sense of everything going away except the person (or people) in the chamber with the Sky and Earth. It induced an immediate and deep sense of calm and peace. It felt as though all troubles and worries could be given to the Earth or Sky there and they were absorbed and the burdens were removed from the human bearer. And, it was quiet! There was something about the shape that reflected outside sound away. It was SO PEACEFUL to sit in there on the bench and watch the sky change up overhead.

I felt the energy was perfect. I considered not putting on a roof. I consulted the Spirits and referred to the recurring vision, and the message I got was "put a roof on it, but leave a large central opening."

Bond Beam

Once the adobes were done, a decision had to be made about the roof. There were a few ideas floating around. There were thoughts about symmetry and design. After playing with different designs, I noticed the doorway was $1/12^{th}$ the circumference of the circle, and I discovered designs with 12 spokes "fit" wonderfully with the door in a way that 3, 4, 6, and 8-way symmetries didn't. A 12 spoke design fit best with the door and it was the winner. All of this felt as though it was guided by some unseen force outside of anyone's conscious mind.

That 12 part roof design defined a wooden "ring" around the top of the wall. It only took a day to custom cut the large pieces of 4" x 10" lumber.

Door Lintel

Up until just before the bond beam, I procrastinated and didn't know what to do with the top of the door. There were options, but looking around the yard, I noticed a big, old, weathered log at the end of the driveway. The log had roughly the same patina as the door posts. I walked past this viga nearly every day and it had become invisible to him. On the day to finish the doorway, though, I noticed it, and upon closer inspection, it looked perfect. It was solid – not rotted at all, and it was long enough. It "spoke" to me about belonging on top of the door.

It was a heavy chunk of wood – 12" in diameter and about 6 feet long. The top of the doorway was just high enough and hard enough to reach that I couldn't do it by himself with my weak back. I had an idea about how to carve the lintel so it could sit on top of the door posts, but it would be tricky to chisel it out carefully and precisely enough to make it look good and be strong.

Luckily, on the next day, Jim came by to help and Jim and I chiseled out holes in the door lintel to make it fit securely on top of the door posts. It took the whole morning with Jim and I both sawing, drilling, and chiseling a little at a time until it fit just right. Jim and I thought we'd need to connect it with screws and adhesive, but, when we put it in place for a fit check and sledgehammered it down, it had no give or budge at all. There was no way it was coming loose. It wasn't going anywhere. And it looked wonderful. It completed the doorway and the ring around the top in a very complementary way.

Roof

After the lintel was on Marie made a good lunch and the three of us, Jim, Marie, and I sat around brainstorming about how to build the roof. We built a little model out of pencils and toothpicks. Jim was so creative and came up with the idea of putting in a central pole and building temporary supports underneath the roof to hold it up as we built.

Jim asked about construction details. "How are you going to attach the roof beams to the bond beam? How are you going to attach the decking to the roof beams? What's going to keep it all from collapsing?" I had to reply, "I don't know." Jim bet me

$50 that the roof wouldn't hold up. Jim thought it would collapse. I took the bet. It was a good challenge.

The next weekend, on Saturday, Mike's friends Jim, Pat, and Corey helped start the roof.

Pat, Corey, Mike, and Jim on June 23th, 2013

The work completed that day –
temporary roof support structure, roof beams, and first ring of decking

Marie and Corey's wife, Lorraine made a great feast to celebrate after the construction that day.

After that, it took just a few more work days to deck the rest of the roof. Jim and I decked about half in one day, and I finished in bits and pieces over the rest of the week.

Another Injury and Message About Slowing Down

I am a slow learner. I tried to get a lot done and work late one evening even though I was tired. On the last cut of the day, as the circular saw blade was slowing to a stop, I leaned on a board that tipped the saw over toward the edge of the roof. In a reflex, I grabbed the saw to keep it from falling into the dirt and I bumped the moving blade with the tip of my finger. It felt like it

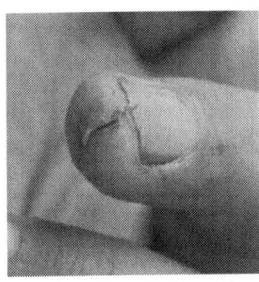

was just "jammed" it but when I looked down, it was bleeding onto the roof boards. It was a minor wound but serious enough that it required a trip to urgent care to get it cleaned and splinted. I kept it clean and wrapped until it healed.

This was another lesson and turning point: first, the Bobcat tipping over on its side, then the back injury, and now the cut finger. What would it take to learn to slow down? For some reason, this time it really hit home and sunk in to a deeper level. After this (at nearly the end of the project though), I learned that if I was starting to get agitated, frustrated, angry, tired, or disappointed AT ALL, I needed to stop right there and get calm before proceeding. So I did. I moved slowly, slower than ever, and stopped, took a breath (or two) and asked myself "What am I doing? What is the purpose?" Any time I got frustrated after that, I waited for it to subside before proceeding. It was a WONDERFUL feeling to be able to do that.

The visioning and construction of this chamber was a type of initiation into a truer, deeper, or larger, more vast self – a self that was not egoically pursuing effectiveness, productivity, or self-aggrandizement, but rather a self with a much larger, and more expansive scope of time and space. And these injuries and setbacks were a necessary part of the process to make me "slow down" and "pay attention" to what really matters instead of just "hurrying up" to "get things done".

Marie had been counseling all along that there should only be "good emotional energy" and "good intentions" going into this structure because it would hold all the energy I put into it. She believed I should be "clear" before I did anything. I understood what she was saying, but I wasn't able to completely clear out my frustration at times, and I felt I shouldn't wait until I was "perfect" before I started anything. For me, I would wait forever if I did that. But, I did agree and was able to learn and practice noticing when I was agitated, then calming myself down, then proceeding after I was clear. That was one of the big lessons during the building of this chamber.

For some reason, this final injury caused a shift and I finally got it. What I got was that when the overly strong emotions came up, I could pause, and clear them right then and there before proceeding. It usually only required a brief pause. In other words, I learned it's an ongoing process for me. And even if I can't clear everything out ahead of time and stay clear mentally and emotionally and expect that to hold at all times, indefinitely, it's OK to proceed anyway as long as that awareness is present, and I at least pause and reflect and get clear as best I can.

Roof - Continued

Pat and I talked about how to strengthen and stabilize the roof structure. I had a vision of a metal ring inside the top of the roof, and independently, in one of our conversations, Pat, who is a mechanical engineer, strongly recommended a continuous metal ring around the inner diameter of the roof, near the central opening. Pat said this continuous metal ring would add lots of strength and rigidity from a structural engineering standpoint. Since I had seen this in a "vision" the night before too, I knew it needed to go in. Pat suggested having the metal ring fabricated by a local metal shop. But, being cheap, I cringed at the anticipated cost, even though the benefit of added strength was clear. Then, the next day, I was looking through my Dad's tools in the barn and saw a conduit bender. Voila - more manna from heaven! I realized I could fabricate the metal ring myself with plain old off-the-shelf electrical conduit and couplers. 3, 10-foot sections would do the trick perfectly. I embedded the ring in notches cut into the roof beams and held the ring in place with decking screwed into the beams from above. So, the metal ring was made that way. It cost less than $10 and I was able to fabricate it the next morning in less than an hour. Plus, it had the added bonus of connecting with my Father and his livelihood. Beautiful!

Finishing the Roof

Our youngest son, Carlos Rael Pedroncelli, surprised us with a visit from San Diego on June 30th. While he was in Albuquerque, he and our middle son, David, came by and helped remove the temporary roof support. David and Carlos loved the chamber and it was great to have them help with that step. The roof held up fine and barely budged. Jim owes me $50. But, I owe Jim way more than that for his consulting and labor… (Just kidding, it's all in fun.)

First Ceremony

On 7/7/2013 at 7:00 PM, Marie and I had the first fire ceremony in the "Circle of Light" Peace Chamber. It was beautiful. Fire ceremonies on the 7th of each month at 7:00 PM local time, are one of the ceremonies Joseph envisioned for the Peace Chambers around the world. On this day, with this ceremony, this Chamber entered into the worldwide community of Chambers.

The chamber did not have a name and Marie and I weren't able to connect with Joseph to get a name from him. So, I felt empowered by Spirit to give it a name and the name that came was "Circle of Light" – one of Joseph's phrases he often uses to describe positive gatherings of people and our own personal and collective consciousness.

Construction Epilogue

The structure of the chamber was finished on June 30th, 2013, two years to the day after groundbreaking with the Bobcat. And the roofing material was completed on July 11th, 2013, on the one year anniversary of my retirement. These dates were not planned. I only noticed them after the fact. And yet, they point to a design that was guided by a larger force. This was definitely a life changing rite of passage and ritual of connection and return.

Joseph's Visit in June, 2015

Joseph visited the chamber in June, 2015 and it was another unforgettable experience.

Joseph was recovering from health issues and was not allowed to venture out and visit people much. But, he heard about the Chamber and he wanted to see it. So, on one of his trips to Albuquerque, he called Marie and I, and asked us to pick him up so he could visit.

I picked him up and he came to the Chamber. He loved it. Marie, Joseph, and I were in the Chamber for about an hour. Joseph was instantly calm and at Peace. I could tell he felt "at home".

As before, when we met him the first time, he was very gentle, polite, and kind. He asked how our day was going and he asked, "*What is going on in your lives?*" We told him we were blessed and grateful and it was a peaceful and abundant time for us with good health, our family doing well, and no major worries. We explained a typical day. I felt calm this time. I felt less "hero worship" and it felt more like a visit with family. He put us at ease and Marie was wonderfully warm, calm, and welcoming, as usual.

He asked us *"What is your experience with this chamber?"* I was nervous for a second, thinking I better say "the right thing", but then I just started talking and it came out OK. I said "It is a place where we feel calm because everything is cleared away and we are here with just the Earth and Sky. We feel the living spirit of Peace alive in us here and we feel it all around – not only in the Chamber but as though the Chamber is everywhere. We feel the Chamber helps us practice being peaceful and connecting to the vast self, which is much greater than our personal selves or problems. We feel a vibration that connects out to a vast distance and far back and forward in time as well. We also feel a beautiful and profound connection with all life and energy here. It feels as important as the gift of life itself. And, it's easy to be grateful here and feel one with All Life and All That Is." He nodded and asked, *"What about you, Marie?"* Marie said, "Me too. I feel peace here. We love it. It's amazing!" [Notice how much more succinct and to the point Marie is than I am. Haha] Joseph nodded again and said *"Yes. That's it, isn't it? That's very good. That's what these chambers are about."*

I asked him about his practices and experiences and what his days are like nowadays. He didn't seem too interested in the question. But, he replied, *"I feel the Peace here too."* He also said, *"Every day's different. But,* **I'm a mystic, so I live from miracle to miracle and prayer to prayer.**" He had the slightest hint of his sly, shy, but contented, grinning expression. I LOVED that expression and what he said!

We sat there in silence for many minutes. All three of us were comfortable sitting in silence in that Chamber together. There was no need for talking.

Then, Joseph looked around at the chamber and he looked at Marie and I and his eyes got big, with a look of surprise. He said *"Yes. This is it!"* We asked "What?" He said, *"In 1953, I had the first vision of a Peace Chamber and this is the Chamber I saw! I've been all over the world and I've seen all the chambers. Each one is different, but this is the one I saw in my first vision of a Chamber. I remember the year because I was 18 years old and the vision came at the end of a Sun Dance ceremony I performed as completion of my training with my grandfather the summer before I had to go to the Indian school in Santa Fe."* We looked at him wide-eyed, with a sense of wonder, and a look of "tell-us-more". He continued, *"At the end of the Sun Dance, I saw a vision of a Kiva with men and women singing and chanting. But, I was just a kid at that time, so I didn't know what it meant."* I was taken aback because I had always heard and read that he had the vision in the 80's. I had never heard about this one before. But, here he was, telling us about it. I asked if he knew that what he was seeing in that vision was a Peace Chamber instead of a Kiva. He said, *"No, I didn't know what it meant then. I thought it was strange. But I always remembered it."* We told him it was a great honor and blessing to be connected to all of it and that it was amazing he saw this Chamber, 60 years before it was built. He nodded approvingly, with an expression that was a mix of astonishment and matter-of-factness, like - Yeah, that's the way it works, sometimes.

I asked Joseph if he knew why the three of us had been chosen to do this together right now, at this moment. After several seconds, he looked at us thoughtfully and replied, *"We've been together a long time, many lifetimes."* He looked down as if checking to see if he should tell us. Then, he looked back up, *"For ... 20,000 years, we've been together. We were together in the First World when everything was in mineral form, then the Second World when there was plant life, then the Third World when there were animals, and then in the Fourth World when humans came together in the first circle of light. People came from the North, and the South, and the East, and the West. But, they didn't call it that, because they each thought they were in the center."* (He said with a mischievous, glinty-eyed, grin.) *"We all gathered together because we wanted to live and work together in peace and harmony. We came together at the beginning of the Fourth World when humans first got together in a circle. And now we came to Earth in this life to meet because we're in the Fifth World where we will live for and with each other, not just for ourselves. That's why they brought us here and we agreed to come this time."*

We sat in silence. After a few minutes, he said, *"Well, I better go back now."* We didn't want the visit to end, but it had to end sometime. As we got up and started walking out, I asked, "Can we have a quick blessing for the chamber before you go?" Joseph said, *"Yes! A blessing would be good."* So, the three of us stood and held hands in the middle of the chamber and Joseph said something like, *"We are here together in Peace just as we have been since the first humans came together in the first circle of light. And, we'll be together again as the last humans on Earth gather in the final circle. But, then we'll be together again somewhere else because there are hundreds of worlds to explore. Aho!"* All three of us were tearing up – misty. We let go of each other's hands and he turned to walk out of the chamber. As he exited the chamber he said, *"It's so beautiful, it makes me want to cry."* We knew he was talking about tears of joy. There was no sadness.

The Life of the Chamber and Connection with Community

Marie and I often spend time in the Chamber. We hold monthly Fire Ceremonies on the 7th. The Chamber has an amazing "Life" and "Spirit" of its own. It's peaceful, yet powerful. Neighbors, friends, and family have visited. There have probably been hundreds of visitors at this point. Most everyone is positive about the space and energy there. Children, young adults, and older people especially love it in there. They seem to "get it" right away. Each person projects and receives their own images, blessings, and healings on and with the the earthen walls and earthen floor and the open sky, the trees and winged creature up above. Everyone walks down the descending dirt path, crosses the threshold, looks at the ground and walls, and ceiling, then stands, sits, or lies down and looks up at the day or night sky. Some people take off their shoes and socks and put their feet on the Earth. Some smell and touch the Earth. Some sing, dance, meditate, or pray in there. There have been tears shed over grief and loss and sorrow. Also, many positive intentions for self-healing and healing of others and the whole Earth and all Life have been requested, hoped, wished, dreamed, and prayed for in there. We have danced, sang, talked, listened, sat in silence, and felt everything that humans can feel in there. **It is a calming, peaceful place and it connects each person with the calming, peacefulness inside themselves, the unity between us, and the vastness of deep space and time, Earth, and Sky. It is elemental, timeless – another world. It is a place of Peace – a sacred space.**

It's also been a blessing to meet others who are connected with Joseph Rael and his followers. Some dear friends and beautiful people come to the fire ceremonies and we have exchanged emails, stories, gifts, blessings, and prayers with people in Joseph's extended "circle of light" all around the world. This is a gift of Spirit that keeps on giving and it feels like it holds the center of a wonderful, lifelong connection to vastness for us. We are grateful.

Also, on a personal level, recently, I realized who or what the spirit that I thought was a guardian angel for the chamber – the spirit that planted the idea in my mind for decades, and the spirit that lovingly encouraged me all along the way – I realized who that spirit was. It was a spirit from the future that came back in time to create this experience for me and any and all energies, people, spirits, and creatures connected and influenced with this chamber. And the guardian angel spirit from the future that came to me in this lifetime to make sure this happened is ***myself from the future!*** In the future, I saw that I could give this gift to myself way back in the past (which was now, in the 2000's) to heal, bless, and expand the consciousness and energy far into the future and past and far out in not only time but also space. I debated whether to share this here because my egoic self is judging it as arrogant. But my soul or spirit self knows it is true and I should share it.

Section 2 - Dreams

Some of the big life events such as growing up with my parents, getting married and having a family, having and leaving a career, and the experiences like those I described where we learned we are Angels by meeting our friend at the end of her life on the bridge, and being connected with Joseph Rael and our chamber and the worldwide chamber community and coming to know my own self as spirit have all been an initiation and opening into a larger awareness. But, there have been smaller, discrete messages that have come in through other channels along the way as well. Many of these messages have come in the form of dreams. This section of the book is about a few of those dreams.

~~~~~~~~~~~~~~~~

I think I inherited a vivid dreaming mind from my Dad, who has amazing, detailed, and symbol-filled dreams that he remembers completely.

As far back as I can remember, I've liked dreams and felt they were important for me. Around age 18 or 20, I read *Carl Jung*'s book, *Memories, Dreams, and Reflections*, and it had a profound effect on me. It opened me up to a mythic, spiritual, and whole life view that was much larger than my Catholic upbringing. Many confirmations, insights, and revelations came alive for me with that book. One thought that struck me was that I should pay attention to my dreams and look for meaningful signs and inner guidance coming from the unconscious mind through the dreams.

I read about Freud's interpretations of dreams too. But, Jung appealed to me much more than Freud. For the most part, Freud's interpretations of symbols didn't resonate or match my inner experience. But, Jung's did.

For a time, I was interested in lucid dreaming and that deepened the dreaming experience. I became aware that I was simultaneously an observer of the dream and a character in the dream. I found that very interesting. I also became aware that many points of view were occurring simultaneously during the dreams. Not only was there the "actor" version of me in the scene, and the impartial "observer", but there was also a morally judging, culturally-conditioned "critic" involved, and also a thinking, comparing, analyzing "evaluator" trying to interpret the meaning of what was happening, and another consciousness, or quality of consciousness, that was like a director, trying to push or pull the action in a specific direction. Sometimes the director would ask questions, or make requests to understand the emotional content more completely. And then there was an overarching "meta" awareness that was aware of all this. I found that fascinating.

It felt like these different points of view were different "characters" or types of consciousness, but the idea also occurred to me that maybe these were all just different qualities or characteristics of one entity and the entity was me. The entity I felt most aligned with was the omniscient, third person, super-consciousness level that had observed and catalogued all the modes of being, thinking, sensing, and feeling (emotions) without making any value judgment. But, I knew all the "lower" types of consciousness with fear, desire, condescending separation, intelligence, and so on, were also aspects of myself. I was as intrigued by the dreamer as the dreams themselves.

In the dreams, and especially when practicing lucid dreaming, it seemed as though there was a heightened awareness compared to ordinary, waking, human consciousness and I liked that too. I was aware of emotions, sounds, smells, tastes, and touch sensations in dreams in addition to pure visuals. And I was aware of other character's sensations in the dreams as well as my own, the actor.

I was interested in the fact that I could "pause" the action and look around, or back up, or attempt to direct the dream. For example, if the actor "I" was going to get hit by a semi-truck, I could stop the truck and move, or look around first. Or, if I was flying around, I could choose to go left, right, forward, backward, up, or down – usually. But, oftentimes, I noticed that when I attempted to steer the dream, it would go in a different direction. When the dream wouldn't go the way I requested, I took that as a significant message in itself.

To this day, I enjoy and believe in the importance of dreams. So, I am telling some of my dreams here that have been important for me. Again, there are many, many dreams. These are just a few. But, these are some highlights that were big for me.

Jumping on the Trampoline

One of the first recurring dreams I remember came back many times from around age ten through my 40's. This dream came a lot when I was younger, then less frequently as I got older - maybe a few times a year, and then a year or two between occurrences toward the end. But it kept coming back. And when it did, it was virtually identical each time, except for gradual, minor changes in the people on the trampoline, and slight elaboration and increased exploration above the clouds in later years. Now, it's just part of me and I can experience it in waking consciousness anytime.

The setting of the dream is in the gym at the local church where I grew up – Our Lady of Guadalupe in Albuquerque. I'm 7 to 10 years old in the dream.

Another person or two and I are jumping on a trampoline and there are a few people waiting to get on and a few more milling around, doing their own things in the gym. Early in my life, the other jumpers were my brothers and childhood friends. Later in life, the other jumpers were often more recent friends, my wife, Marie, or our kids.

Two or three of us start jumping and with every jump, we get higher and higher. The other jumpers don't jump very high or for very long before they stop and get off the trampoline or they bounce awkwardly and jump off or fall off. But, surprisingly, I stay in the middle of the trampoline, and I keep jumping. The other people are laughing or saying "Hey look at him! Be careful." I'm not self-conscious or awkward about it. I feel an ease and grace. I'm calm, comfortable, and unafraid.

I jump higher and higher until I'm almost hitting my head on the ceiling of the gym – maybe 20 feet high. I have a moment of concern about hitting my head, but then I notice the ceiling has opened up and I'm able to go even higher. I'm bouncing 10, 20, 50, then hundreds, and even thousands of feet above the gym. I'm getting so high, that I begin to notice it takes many seconds, maybe even a minute to get up and then an equal amount of time to come back down to Earth on each bounce. I get so high that I can see the whole neighborhood, and even the whole city and surrounding landscape.

Then, I start getting close to the clouds. I keep bouncing higher until I'm above the clouds. It's still pleasant and fun. After I'm bouncing up above the clouds, I don't go any higher. The highest I get is just a little above the clouds. At the top of each bounce, there's a feeling of weightless floating for a few seconds. On about the third bounce above the clouds, I get the feeling I could just stop and rest on top of the clouds instead of falling back down. So, on the next bounce, I do it! I stop and rest on top of the clouds. I lie down, or sometimes walk around, up there. It's peaceful and quiet. After a while, whenever I feel I'm ready, I let myself fall back down through the clouds.

The first several times I had this dream, I walked around looking for the exact spot I came up, worried that I'd have to be at the same spot to fall down or I might miss the trampoline. But, I'm disoriented up there. It's puffy and white and it all looks the same. But, I fall back down and I magically drift to the trampoline on the way down. After a few times of this, I don't worry about it when I get up there because it's familiar and I know I'll return to the trampoline on the way down.

After I'm done up on the clouds, I allow myself to fall through the clouds and I fall all the way down to the trampoline where I bounce up and down some more. But after I come down from the clouds, I bounce lower and lower each time until I'm finally standing on the trampoline. The hole in the roof of the gym closes up. I step off and other people take their turns. Some of them tell me "You were bouncing a long time. We thought you weren't coming back. It's about time you give us a chance."

I loved this dream for a long time but I never thought much about it other than that it was pleasant. Then, one time a friend asked me if I had any recurring dreams that I thought were important in my life. Out of the blue, this one popped into my head and I told him about it. He loved it too and we both tried to analyze what it might mean. We thought it had to do with exploring broader vistas than the family, church, and neighborhood view of things – and going all the way up to heaven to see what it was like up there.

One great aspect of it was that it was all safe and OK. I was able to control the heights and return back to the ordinary, Earthly realm upon request. So, it also had to do with being able to move back and forth between heaven and earth with comfort, and ease.

It remains a powerful and comforting metaphor of life and even death for me.

Mature Self Meeting Younger Male Self

This dream came only once, in my early 50's. I had been thinking about and working a lot on my relationship with my father. I had a rough, distant, and disappointing relationship with him. He was a mildly abusive alcoholic in the years when I lived in his household. He was quick to judge and express disappointment and disagreement. He didn't seem to respect anyone and much of anything. And even at the time of this dream, at a much advanced age, he didn't express much affection or appreciation toward or about me. He seemed to be focused on his own needs and not able to give or care much about others. It bothered me because I saw an echo of all these qualities in myself. I wished I could "heal" or "fix" him, or at least have some kind of healing about our relationship.

I knew his external lashing out at others had to do with his bad feelings about himself and I felt bad that he felt so bad and took it out on others.

For the most part, I had given up expecting anything different from him since the time I was a teenager. But, I still wanted to be able to accept and forgive him and myself for not being able to live any other way than the way we had. I had a need to go deeper into the grief of never having had a father I wish I could have had. And I also had a need to just move on and be OK with myself, who I was and how the fathering, and lack thereof, had impacted me and how I am as a father myself.

That was the background of this dream.

In the dream, I met myself. One of "me" was the current "me", a 50-some year old greying, calm, kind, patient, wise and caring, but also restless, weary, normal, fallible man. And the other "me" was about 7 years old, a polite, attentive, curious, interested, engaging and engaged, but also somewhat anxious and nervous kid. The two me's greeted each other with surprise, but warmly, with gentle kindness, happy expectation, eager appreciation, and genuine interest and concern for each other.

The older me said to the younger me something like, "Is there anything you would like to ask me?"

The younger me said something to the effect of, "What's it going to be like for me in the future? Will everything be OK? Will I be OK?"

The older me kneels down to the height of younger me, puts an arm around younger me, and says, "Everything will be OK. You'll be a kind, wise, and patient person. You'll meet lots of good people, and you'll be a good person and positive influence to many people. You'll become just like me, and it'll be really good. In fact I am you."

At that moment, the older "I" was letting the younger "myself" know that the only adequate father I could ever have was my own "inner" father. I had to cultivate and develop that inner, mature, whole, and healthy fathering principle in myself and over time, I did. At that meeting of the younger and older versions of "me", the healthy father "me" healed the wounded child "me", and the healing of the child, healed any remaining resentment, bitterness, and any other woundedness that was still in the adult. There was complete forgiveness.

In that instant, I felt a direct connection in time, as if time collapsed between young and old. And I felt all the pain in that time span evaporate, and disappear. I knew *in that instant, that the "father wound" and the "child wound" were healed for me going forward as well. I knew that I had been providing and receiving adequate fathering for myself all along. The younger self knew into the future and the older self knew into the past that the father in me, although developing over time, would be and was wonderful, the whole time.*

The young me got everything he needed to go forward for the rest of his life with a sense of confidence, comfort, and security. And the older me got a fulfilling sense of "doing good" for the kid, and he saw in the kid an openness, desire to know and understand, a curiosity, and sense of awe and wonder that was so alive in the young boy. By experiencing this in the young boy, the old man remembered that all these qualities were still alive in him and, in a flash, the old man re-ignited and re-integrated those aspects of himself into his old man's mind and life. Both of them, the old man and the young boy, were completed by each other. They were no longer separate, but were merged into one.

This dream created a significant shift for me. I felt a lot better in my walking, talking, and feeling, waking life after that. I had a LOT more forgiveness and compassion for my biological father after that dream. And, I had appreciation for the innate desire and drive in me that sought healing for this. Also, I had respect and gratitude for the decency and goodness in myself and even the purity and open, raw, unhealed woundedness in my father.

There has been a different, more open, and patient quality in my relationship with my father since this dream. He's still alive – just turned 80. We live in separate houses on the same property. And we're still working out our respective roles, differences, and finding a deepening relationship with each other. We accept each other for who we are a lot more now, and have far fewer expectations and judgments. Soon after that dream I told my Dad "I love you" for the first time since I was a kid, and he told me "I love you" for the first time I remembered since I was a kid. It was a lot like the dream, except between two of us, and in real life.

A week or two after this "older me meets younger me" dream, I had a similar dream. Except, this time, the younger me was a female. The female person wasn't the physical "me" of this lifetime, but she represented the "young, feminine principle" in me.

I won't recount the details of the dream here, but I do want to say that the second dream with the current aged, male me, meeting a young feminine principle in "me", was a powerful companion dream to the first and together, the two dreams changed my acceptance and forgiveness of all perceived faults or problems in myself from youth to the present.

Since these dreams, I've been the elder for myself that I had long sought to meet in someone else. And the curious, playful, open, aware, innocent, pure, masculine *and* feminine child full of of awe and wonder has been alive and accessible in me as well.

I am softer and more open with others and myself after these dreams. I no longer needed to deny feelings of wanting trust and connection with others, and I no longer need to fear that having or showing these feelings will make me vulnerable or weak. I know I am OK having these feelings and letting them flow because I know I am capable of comforting and nurturing myself and there have been and will be others along the way who can feel, acknowledge, and reciprocate these feelings and needs when they come along.

Soul's Creation, "Spiritual Friend", I Am the Path, and the Illumination

Another significant dream:

> *"I" (or some observer, who knows who) am standing on the bank of a wide river looking up at the night sky. A tiny spark of light appears in the night sky as if the light had just poked through the background curtain of blackness. The observer notices it right away and I think "how amazing" that the observer happened to see it just as it first appeared. It gets bigger and brighter and traces a curved path toward the Earth – kind of like a pop fly baseball, but originating in outer space. It seems as though this spark has come from far, far, away - from the center or other side of this galaxy or maybe even another galaxy. In a matter of a few seconds, the spark of light comes all the way down to the Earth, crosses the river, and comes to a stop right in front of a path next to the river.*
>
> *It's like a falling star, and as it gets closer, "I" see that it's coming straight towards me. I have a moment of panic, wondering, will I be burned up if this meteor lands on me. But, I'm far more curious than concerned. I "figure" it will miss me anyway, and if it does kill me, there's nothing I can do about it. I'll just have to watch and wait until the last second to see how close it gets. As it gets closer, I can see it's not very big, and it's not a meteor, it's just pure light.*

Then, the point of view shifts from a ground-based observer, to a point of view that's inside the falling light. Inside that light is elation! There's an excitement and curiosity and amazement about the experience of being in the light as it travels through space and comes to rest at that spot next to the river on the surface of Earth where the original observer was standing!

Then, the point of view shifts to a place above and behind the light. The light has no form or substance. It just radiates out. There's no light bulb, or lamp or anything.

The light doesn't know where to go, or what to do. It doesn't know how to move, or if it should move or in which direction. The light feels it's supposed to go forward and have specific experiences with some aspects of Earth and life on Earth, but it doesn't know which direction has the proper experiences and people and other lights it's supposed to meet with.

Next, a tall, dark shadow appears next to the light. The shadow doesn't have any menacing or worrisome energy. It just looks visually darker than the light. Plus, it has a distinct, tall shape. It seems to be about as tall as the radius of the light, or twice as tall as the center of the light. For a second "I" think it's a light pole and the light is coming from a lamp that's attached to it. But, I can't see any bulb. The dark shape seems to move and shift and change shape. The light and the shadow seem to be involved in some kind of back and forth communication. The light is asking the dark questions and the dark is kindly answering and explaining. Sometimes the dark leans over to the light, or shrinks down to be closer in size and less intimidating to the light. Sometimes, it seems to have a robed, human-like shape. It becomes clear that this is no ordinary lamp pole. In fact, it's not a lamp pole at all.

The light orb and the tall, alternatingly robed then pole-like shadow communicate back and forth for a while. The light is always diffuse and amorphous, but it changes from spherical to slightly oblong in height, or flat and wider from side to side when it asks or receives answers from the shadow. The light changes its vibration and brightness too. The light is mostly white with a beautiful, soft, subtle golden hue.

After a while, the light seems to have its questions answered and it begins moving forward on a path paralleling the river. The shadow follows behind the light. The shadow is never far away.

As the light progresses on its path, it occasionally has doubts and questions about which way to go and what to do next. It asks the shadow if it's on the right path. The shadow conveys, wordlessly, that any choice the light makes will be OK, but the light gets to choose and the shadow will stay with the light. The shadow lets the light know it will be as near and visible, or distant and invisible as the light chooses. But the shadow will show up any time, on a moment's notice, if the light summons it.

This goes on for a while and I become aware that years have passed. The light has made its way and it has reconnected with the shadow off and on throughout its journey. The light has encountered other lights and many interesting scenarios and situations along its way. The light reconnects with the shadow as a kind of culmination of their meetings and after some question *and answer, the light tells the shadow telepathically, "I think I've figured it out. All these years, I thought you (the shadow) were providing the light for me to illuminate my path. But, I think I have realized that I Am my own light! Is that right?" The shadow confirms that is correct by disappearing, letting the light see the shadow disappear, and then letting the light see that there is still light - coming from itself. Then the light requests for the shadow to reappear. The shadow reappears and the light says to the shadow, "And, as far as my 'right path' is concerned, I think that works the same way. I think wherever I go, whichever path I choose, I am providing my own illumination and the extent of that illumination is the full extent of everything I'm supposed to experience and know and understand. So, wherever I go I see and know a little more about where I should go and what I should do next. Is that right?" The shadow let the light know that was right. The light had a big 'Aha' and realized that the extent of his light provided the illumination of just as much as he was supposed to see to allow him to make his next choice and next move forward along the journey.*

The phrase "I AM the Path, I AM the Illumination, and I AM the Awareness" came into the dream. Path was the time and spaces and places travelled. Illumination was the event, sensory, mental and emotional horizon from moment to moment. Path and Illumination worked together in concert. Illumination showed the next way forward along the path and movement along the Path made new things visible to the light. The Awareness was the pure, raw experiencing, but also the accumulation of that experience into learning, and also understanding of the meaning of the experience. Awareness worked back and forth with Illumination and the Path as well. Awareness had to do with choosing what to hold and what to let go and where to go next. But, Awareness was guided and instructed by Illumination and the Path itself. That trio of Path, Illumination, and Awareness affected and interacted with each other and comprised one whole together.

Right away, I thought this was a lot like the saying attributed to Jesus "Ego sum via, veritas, et vita", or "I AM the Way, the Truth, and the Light". And it was also like the Hindu term Sat-Chit-Ananda – which means Being-Awareness-Bliss, and Joseph Rael's Breath-Matter-Movement.

In the moment of the dream, I understood what all that meant.

I felt profoundly grateful for the entity that appeared as a "shadow". I felt it was a kind, patient, expansive counsel "in the shadow", or background, of all my choices, and my understanding, and my journey. It was a WISE companion to me. It helped me. I did not help it. It did not need me (the light). It was a manifestation of all that could be created. It was patient and calm in its service to me throughout my existence as a Light on Earth. I felt this shadow was similar to the concepts of "guardian angel", "spirit guide", or "soul friend".

I also had the sense that this was a parable or metaphor for my soul coming into being on Earth and having an eternal friend and guide that patiently encouraged me to have my own experiences within the sphere of the illumination. The Illumination was how far I could see and hear and understand, and the path was the course of that illumination over time. Amen!

Cigar Shaped Museum 100,000 Years in the Future

Another significant dream happened only one time:

> *I am standing outside of some futuristic looking high-rise building. The building is in the middle of a big, open area, not in an urban environment. I check my watch because I'm waiting to meet some guests who are visiting. I am some sort of tour guide, curator, or senior administrator involved with this building (although I have other places I travel and other jobs I do, as well). But, I have been associated with this building for a long time, and it will soon be time for me to move on to other jobs. So, these guys who are coming to visit are younger gentlemen who are interested in possibly filling my role and some of them may someday be the future caretakers, curators, planners, administrators, and guides for this place just as I have been.*
>
> *The guests arrive. I am their tour guide today and these guys have come to meet me and see what I have to show and tell them. I am someone like a university professor, or something like that, and these guys are advanced students of the same subject matter. We know of each other, but this is the first time we've met in person. All of us are happy to meet for the first time. For some reason, they are short on time and have only an hour or two to spend with me at this place.*
>
> *I tell them it's a real treat to have them here and to be able to show them this amazing museum. I suggest we waste no more time with social nicety and superficial pleasantries and we get right into the museum. They're excited to jump in.*

We enter the building, and it's simple and elegant. There's a small lobby, maybe 30 feet by 30 feet in size with two elevators. There are few visitors there and almost no wait to get an elevator. As we get in, I explain to the guys that there's an incredible wealth of collected material and history in this building, but I want to make sure we hit some specific highlights in this, their first, but brief, tour.

I tell them I'd like to take them to the second floor first. I explain that the museum is arranged chronologically, with the older eras on the lower floors and more recent eras on top. So, we're going to an "old" level first. They say "Whatever you recommend will be great for us. You're the one who knows this place."

At the second floor, we get off and only stay a few minutes. It's a harsh, dry, dusty, but beautiful natural environment. It goes for miles in each direction and the guys are amazed that it's so large. The ceiling is very high as well. It's so high, that we can't really see where it stops. The guys ask what time period this represents and I cryptically tell them it's an "early time" before humans. They're knowledgeable and they discuss amongst themselves about the current scholarship of when these conditions may have existed on earth and how accurate this depiction may be. They are pretty confident they know all about it and they don't ask many questions, so I don't say much.

Next, we go to the tenth floor. The tenth floor is like a conventional, 21st century museum. It has high ceilings and looks like the inside of a well-lit building. We start making our way around. There are incredible examples

91

of art and culture from different regions around the world. There are huge, stylized statues, dioramas, and specimens like mummies and taxidermies of humans, animals, and plant life, and delicate works of daily living items – things like shoes, clothing, pots, and urns – but made with amazing, detailed, creative, and artful workmanship. Lots of the artwork depicts scenes of villages and natural settings with people living there. There is an amazing variety of living arrangements on land and water in these artworks, with everything from sparse populations close to nature to dense clustering in villages and urban settings. It seemed like it was a grouping of "antique" civilizations and cultures like Viking, Celt, Persian, Mongolian, Ottoman, Turk, Egyptian, Inca, Maya, Aztec, Greek, and Roman-level cultures all represented together on this floor. But, these appeared to be some of the best examples of all of these civilizations together in one place on this floor.

One piece I draw their attention to is a sculpture that seems to be carved out of a single, solid piece of dark, shiny stone. It's enormous, maybe 9 feet tall, by 25 feet long and 12 feet deep. The first impression as one approached was its enormity and the beauty and uniformity of the polished stone. Then, as one got closer, one could see the tremendous detail, realism, and extraordinary craftsmanship of the carving. The carving depicted daily life in what appeared to be a pre-technology culture. There were people in their homes and in communal areas working and playing in their villages in the hills and other people living, working, and playing down at the edge of water. Some people were fishing from the shore, hauling in and sorting out their catch. Others were in boats. There were waves and rocks and hills and trees and plants in the carving. And there were animals on the mountainside in the vegetation and in and around the clusters of villages. The figures were maybe an inch or two tall and there were thousands of figures in the sculpture. It went on and on. We walked around the sides and found the back side was just as detailed. We marveled at the workmanship and the commitment to create and complete such an elaborate work to document this culture's way of life. We were amazed by the size of it too. We wondered how it was even transported into this building. We only looked at a small fraction of the whole area, and a half hour, or so, had already passed. So, I advised the young men that even though it would be richly rewarding to spend the whole time here, I thought they would want to see some of the other floors. They said OK.

 We worked our way back to the elevators and went to a middle floor, maybe 68, or so. On that floor, it was a futuristic metropolis. There were flying vehicles and floating buildings. We watched from a platform that was jutting out in mid-air. The guys were astonished that we were still in the building. They asked how big the building was. I told them it was many miles high. Each floor was anywhere from 100 feet to two miles tall and the whole building was shaped like a cigar standing on end. The lower floors were smaller, maybe a mile or two in diameter, but some of the upper and upper-middle stories were 30 to 50 miles in diameter. I told them this museum was built to house replicas of these different eras and patterns of human habitation. They were *astounded and asked how such a large structure could have been constructed. What were the materials of the structure? How is it heated and cooled and supplied with fresh air? What organization or organizations funded, designed, built, and organized all this? Who maintains it? And other administrative questions like that. I told them that it was a consortium of the whole human race and all life that decided it was important to preserve this for future generations so that none of it would be forgotten. I told them not to get too caught up in the governance and technical issues of the museum for now. They could study that later. For now, they should just enjoy it all and marvel at being here.*

We hailed an air taxi on the 68th floor and flew around the city for a quick tour. We were running low on time, so I strongly suggested we take in one more floor. The guys agreed.

I took them to the 102nd floor. I told them 102 was near the top. The museum currently had 104 floors, but was designed in such a way that additional floors could be added when (or if) they were needed.

When we stepped out on the 102nd floor, it appeared to be an entirely natural environment with vegetation something like a rain forest. From our perch atop the edge of a cliff we could see miles away out to the horizon where there was a brilliant sunset. We couldn't be sure, but it seemed like we could barely make out the glass walls at the edge of the museum miles away. We sat there in wordless awe and wonder at the primordial sight. The vegetation was similar to modern vegetation but it seemed different than anything from the modern world. The men's minds fell silent. There were a few *sounds of animals and some wind, and thunder, but no signs of human habitation. The men and I had no need to talk because we were able to communicate telepathically. The visitors asked me if this was more recent than the eras with the elaborate artworks and the futuristic city. I replied that it was. They asked what happened to the advanced civilizations that led to this situation. I explained that the population had decreased substantially and Earth restored itself to something that was similar to the primeval Earth. I told them that this museum was a biosphere and each floor replicated the atmospheric conditions and preserved the lifeforms of each epoch. They understood. They asked if this was in the future. I explained that this era was 100,000 to 200,000 years after the birth of Christ. After this there weren't any more normal, verbal, question and response answers. Rather, there was a real fast exchange of information back and forth with hundreds or thousands of thought forms, ideas and connected streams of interest and knowledge exchanged almost instantaneously.*

They perceived that "I" was letting them know, but it was all coming from the grand intelligence. They wondered about the next two levels. Were those even further in the future? What are they like – densely or sparsely populated? Does humanity become extinct? When? What was the time frame of the first floors? What were they like – primitive or futuristic? Answers were given.

The gist of it was that this museum represented hundreds of thousands to even millions (or billions?) of years of human, plant, animal, and environmental

> history, and it was designed and built in such a way that it could preserve historically significant eras far into the past and future. This suggested that the "governing" or overall, managing intelligence would preserve something in the future as well.
>
> We got back in the elevator and went down to the ground floor. When we got to the bottom floor, we stepped back and looked up and saw how huge the building was. We also noticed it was floating above the ground. The visitors got into their futuristic, air taxis to go to the airport where they were getting a flight to somewhere else.
>
> Right before the dream ends, I get the sense that this museum was created and is being maintained by a "future" civilization that is tasked with archiving this history and keeping the various strains of life intact.

This dream showed me that plants, animals, and the Earth environment go through significant changes over time and there have been and will be times when human existence is almost non-existent. I was shown the "lifecycle" of species and the biological environments over vast stretches of time, but I was given the perspective of a caretaker or curator who was able to see it all with a fond, loving nostalgia and sense of respect, but not too strong an emotional sentimentality about it.

I noticed that the upper floor, 102, was similar to the lower floor, 2. And I was fairly sure that some of the intermediate floors looked to be purely natural and mostly devoid of humans as well. I also noticed that even in the 10th floor, although the artifacts seemed to be "ancient", they were also more advanced than any artifacts we know about in the 21st century. I thought the 21st century was probably between the 2nd and the 10th floor.

I wondered about time and the advancement and progressive complexity of human intelligence and ingenuity. It looked like a lot of the "primitive" eras were advanced and the "primeval" eras of the past were just like future time periods after human populations declined. It occurred to me that **100,000 years in the past was about the same as what it will be like 100,000 years in the future and there are ebbs and flows that are cyclic and recurring in terms of humans, or human-like life and the rest of the natural world.**

I left the dream convinced that human beings will survive long into the future, but have experienced, and will continue to experience significant diebacks.

After this dream, my relationship with time changed. When I had concerns after this dream, I found myself asking "Was this thing I'm concerned about matter in the past? Will it matter 1, 10, or 100 years in the future? How about 1,000 years? 10,000? 100,000? Will this be important in 1 million years? How about 1 billion years?

I noticed that I often envisioned Earth, the water, atmosphere, and all plant, animal, and human life far into the past and future after this dream. I even had visions and dreams that showed me these kind of cycle on galactic and cosmic scales. In one vision, I experienced that even the creation and completion of each galaxy over billions of years through events like big bangs are relatively benign and small scale events in the even grander scheme of things. The birth and death of cosmos was shown to me as in breaths and out breaths of some grander spirit, or consciousness.

After this dream my personal worries, cares, and desires seemed so small and insignificant. This is a great help to me.

1 Photon From 100,000 Light Years Away

The night of 11/11/2016, I had three nice "visions" in a dream. They were scenes that just flashed in for a second each. Here's what I wrote in my dream journal:

> *The first was a scene with Donald Trump surrounded by a bunch of people. It was kind of like a view of a video for a fraction of a second. The TV-like-view receded into the distance until I could no longer see it.*
>
> *The second image was the chamber, but it had a big ball over the opening in the roof.*
>
> *I was given the message that the big crystal-ball-like feature above the chamber was some kind of lens or collector of energy – cosmic energy.*
>
> *The third part of the images-as-vision was a narrow ray of light coming down like this:*

The ray in the third image wasn't connected to the ball over the chamber from the second image in one visual image all together, but I *knew* it was connected *conceptually, like this:*

Taken together, the three images were a beautiful roadmap: first, I will receive the gift of being able to "zoom out" and away from Trump and American politics. I will have the luxury of not needing to concern myself about it too much since it will pass and the effects will ebb and flow into something else, but none of it is "my job".

Next, my focus was directed to the energy lens of the chamber. This ties in with dreams I've been having for the last month or so of just being in the chamber. The chamber has an energetic life of its own but I can go in there too and receive and give – coexist, and be in the life and energy field of the chamber.

This is a particularly special gift since the chamber is a lens that connects and concentrates cosmic energy.

The third part, with the rays from above has to do with collecting starlight (including sunlight – the sun is a star.) In the vision, I seemed to "ask for" and "be given" answers about what these images mean. The answers came right after the visual images and they came "wordlessly" but with very rich and full explanation of meaning.

The meaning of the third part is that the chamber has to do with observing and collecting cosmic energy. I felt the chamber was a big eyeball and the environment created by the structure allowed human consciousness to "sense" particles coming in that were billions of years old and coming from vast distances. The phrase I got was that **the chamber allows us to understand that we are able to receive and perceive energy as subtle as "1 photon from 100,000 light years away"**.

I woke up, looked at the clock and the time was

I interpreted the three 4's as 3 medicine wheels stacked on top of each other. 12 = heaven + human + earth medicine wheels, maybe?

[I think my conscious mind may have made that part up and you can tell because it doesn't have the same power as the rest.]

Anyway, I think all the medicine wheel stuff came from the time and space proximity with Joseph Rael and David Kopacz at the talk and book signing for "Walking the Medicine Wheel" at the Bookworks bookstore, down the road from our house and the chamber, which had happened the night before.

After I woke up, I spent the whole morning learning about the human eye and I saw how it's like the vision of the ball on the kiva:

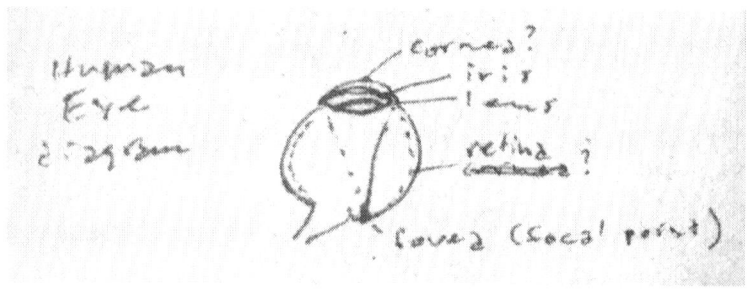

I read up about how sensitive the human visual system is. It turns out it <u>can</u> detect a single photon. Also, I read up about how far away the stars are that we can see with our naked eyes, with binoculars, and with telescopes. It turns out most of the stars in the night sky are in our own Milky Way galaxy and the next nearest bright galaxy - Andromeda. Andromeda is also visible in perfect viewing conditions to people with extremely good vision.

The Milky Way is 100,000 light years in size. We can see stars from our own galaxy up to 100,000 light years away and we can see 1 photon. So, the phrase 1 photon from 100,000 light years away is accurate for the human perceptual sensitivity. Not only is that true, but we can see, with the naked eye, light from much farther. The Andromeda galaxy is 2.5 million light years away!

In addition to what we see, there are other ancient, energetic particles that pass through our bodies. We can "feel" these particles and vibrations and they have an effect on our cells. These particles/waves/quantum packets of matter and energy are ancient and powerful. They are our ancestral raw material. We are made of the same stuff as the stars and our bodies are still being affected and responding to cosmic energy from other galaxies and the whole universe.

~~~~~~~~~~~~~~~

The overarching message of this dream is to "expand one's perspective", and to become aware, and be present with the incredible sensitivity and fullness of one's ability to receive and perceive subtle amounts of energy that are delivered from vast reaches of time and space. Our bodies are made of this same matter and energy that continues to flow to us from vast expanses of time and space. This is a gift and roadmap for a personal journey over the next brief time in this body/mind/spirit (all one!).

John's Message

This is from a dream journal entry.

One of my dearest friends and favorite people I've ever known passed away suddenly in his mid-50's and his life and death shook me and woke me up in a very good way.

The dream happened on April 5, 2015, the 10th anniversary of John Baugh's death. I had been thinking about John off and on in the weeks and days leading up to this anniversary. On the actual anniversary day I thought about him some too, but I was not fixated or obsessed. At some level, though, I think I was wishing for contact with John. I feel I subconsciously asked him to come to me in a dream or connect with me in some way on that day.

That night, I had this dream about John.

We were in a men's group and John was speaking. He was talking very clearly and passionately with great sensitivity and insight. As is his way, he was brilliant but also humble, modest, playful, and funny. He was deeply happy to be talking about what he was talking about. He was telling us how, for most of his life, he had a resistance to looking at death because he didn't know what it was. He said it wasn't really a fear, but it was more of a sense he wouldn't be allowed to know what happened at death and he would find it too frustrating to focus on it, so he avoided it. But, he said, once he died he found that death is really nothing at all. Death is not the end of a person, and birth is not the beginning of the person, they're both just mundane, normal experiences that are part of a continuum of being. He said he now knew that the death experience was fun, interesting, and consciousness expanding, but nothing to be afraid of or avoid. He said it's like going on a vacation, or seeing a different movie, or having a different kind of dream than ever before, so it is a new experience and it does change a person, but the person is still the same core person as before – there's a continuity.

When John paused, I said "Wait. Didn't you die? Aren't you dead? How can I believe what you're saying if you're not even real? Am I just imagining you – are you a figment of my imagination, or are you a real spirit who is now able to appear in physical form for our benefit? How does this work? How do I know I'm not just imagining this version of you in this particular experience?" John paused for a bit and looked at me with an impish, mischievous grin, as if giving me a chance to think about it and get the answer on my own without having to hear words from him. I wasn't "getting it", so John said "Of course you're imagining me, AND, I AM real. Everything you 'experience' and 'know' are memories of your imagination, or imagined approximations of your memories. Everything is a projection of your own preferences and desires to help remember what you already know and create what you need. Even when you're experiencing a person who is 'alive' in their body, you're not really experiencing the total reality of the person, you're mostly framing them in a way that you can understand and feel comfortable with. Sometimes that means keeping the other person at a distance and labeling them as 'other'. Other times it means recognizing the other person as a universal being that has the same characteristics and is made from the same stuff as you. In other words, sometimes you experience the other person as not being separate or different than you. More often than not, most of us are creating our own experience by labeling it, categorizing it, comparing it, and contrasting it to something we think we already "know". This is very different than being completely open to whatever the "*it*" is that is right there in front of us – even if it's strange, unusual, makes no sense, and doesn't compare to anything we've experienced before. Often, we make these comparisons and labeling, putting things in categories like "same" or "different" when we're experiencing something new.

What John just said made my mind explode and I was looking downward and inward, thinking, and trying to "understand" what John had just said so I could figure out what to ask John next to continue the conversation. I said, "So, I am creating this experience of you, but you're also 'real'?" and when I looked up, John was gone. He was no longer sitting in the circle. Yet, I felt he was still present. I felt he was playing hide and seek with me and having fun watching me struggle with it. At that point I started communicating with him telepathically. I'm not sure if I said it out loud or in my mind, but I said something like, "OK, John. I get it. Please come back, I want to talk to you some more and ask you more questions. PLEASE come back into the circle. I know you can if you want to. Just a little more, please?" And an idea came into my mind. I felt it wasn't my idea that I generated, but rather it came into my mind from outside myself. It was a message from John saying "I've said what I wanted to say to you and you've heard what you needed to hear. I've given you plenty to work with, and see – we are still communicating. I don't *have to appear to you in a physical form and make sound that your physical ears can hear. We can communicate directly with thought forms."* Again, my mind was blown. *I was trying to formulate the next thought and continue the conversation, but some part of my mind had resistance, and I was having the same self-talk and self-doubt about "How do I know this isn't real and I'm just imagining it?" So, the opening in me to this telepathic communication just shut down, and I went into my "normal" mind and tried to remember and analyze this dream.*

The dream happened in the middle of the night, and I woke up because I wanted to remember it, but I also wanted to go back to sleep because I was really tired. At first I only remembered the part when John was incarnate. But later the next day, the memory of the dream came back, and that's when I remembered or received the part about the telepathic communication part that happened after John disappeared.

This dream was profound for me. I am very grateful for John appearing with this message. This is a centrally important lesson and truth to some of my deepest recurring questions – "What happens at death? What is reality? What is the function and nature of imagination versus 'real' experience?" This has all the answers to those questions. Our consciousness creates, or imagines, and remembers, that which we need and that which we're ready for. Sometimes it's a little bit at a time, not as much as we want or think we need, but as much as we actually need and are ready for. But, ultimately our experience of reality is something we imagine and remember based on what we are able to hold and what we need. It's a whole different spin on "the Now".

Section 3 - Past Lives

For most of my life, I didn't give much thought to the idea of reincarnation, and when I did, I was skeptical and doubtful at best. But, during the late 2000's and into the early 2010's, I had a growing and recurring interest that became an intense yearning for direct experience of a past life.

Earlier in life, on and off, I had dreams with content that came from beyond anything I knew about or anything I had experienced directly. I felt these scenes and images were "not from my own mind". Plus, I had experienced waking "dreams" or "visions" a few times before – especially related to Joseph Rael and the Sound Chamber. But, the frequency and intensity of these kinds of dreams and visions increased during this time period in the early 2000's. I had many extended, detailed, vivid dreams and visions involving distant times, places, and people. And I also began to meet and read about other people who had similar experiences. All this led me to become more interested in reincarnation and past lives.

My "logical" mind was interested in reincarnation and past lives because it was a possible explanation for the experiences I had. But, the interest itself, was a kind of "non-ordinary" experience too. I couldn't explain or understand why I had this interest. I didn't know why I wanted to follow it. It didn't make sense to me. It was more like it was following me or "it" was choosing me.

I had a thought that instead of reincarnation, another possible explanation for these experiences could be that there's some kind of telepathic stream or storehouse of consciousness where the experience of others is available to any or all – kind of like a big library or party line where anyone's thoughts and memories could be accessed by anyone else. But, I have not found anyone talking about something like this. The closest I've heard in that vein is Carl Jung talking about "collective unconscious", which has to do with archetypal patterns that we all experience. But, my experiences were different than archetypal, or mythic experiences. My experiences were very specific, detailed scenes and memories and lots of them were mundane, but beautiful in their simplicity and ordinariness. I've also heard new age teachers, speakers, and writers talk about the "Akashic records", but everything I've seen and heard talked about there, seems to infer that we each have access to only our own "records", not everyone's. The Akashic idea was a subset of what I felt I was experiencing. I felt that I was shown experience and events from other souls' records.

[At risk of belaboring the point, I don't think all experiences are "personal". I think there is a type of vision that is not tied to one being, or soul, or consciousness, or person. I think all of our experiences are something any and all of us can tap into and experience. But, there is privacy, and free will, too. And the only way we receive information from, for, and about others is if their soul chooses to share it and it's for the greatest good of all involved. This is my current understanding.]

Anyway, these non-ordinary, dreaming and waking experiences that puzzled me and piqued my curiosity so much were as vivid and detailed as normal waking consciousness, and often even more vivid with more details and omniscience or awareness of the other entities in the scene than normal, waking consciousness. For example, as I described with dreams, I could often know other people's thoughts and feelings in these remembered scenes, or be exquisitely aware of plants, animals, the air, earth, or weather.

I wondered why these particular memories or experiences that were so laden with feeling and meaning were popping into my mind and I kept coming back to the idea that past lives could be an explanation for these experiences and I "felt" some knowledge of past lives might help me heal my personal past and visualize the future.

I was not disappointed. In fact, as I followed this line of interest, I had good "opening" or "expansion" of consciousness that far exceeded anything I imagined going in.

In early to mid 2010's, I "let go" of my conscious, logical, culturally-conditioned mind's resistance and I opened up to exploring and experiencing past lives.

In this section of the book, I share some of the highlights of what I believe are a few of my past lives. The past lives I share here are listed as they are presented in the book, which is in reverse chronological order (most recent lives first):

1. Thomas – a young male, growing from ages 10 to 17 with his Nanny, sister, and Father; includes details of his temperament and environment; follows his growing interest in the larger world, and an unquenchable desire for experience on the open ocean.
2. Amara – helper, guide, worker, priestess in seaside all-female community; brief descriptions of how she led spiritual ceremonies; met her guardian spirit in a cave near the ocean; and was killed by thieves in the woods. [Life Between Lives]
3. Kongar – Mongolian king/warlord, killed in battle, beheaded and made an example. [Life Between Lives]
4. Chokrel – An ancient, primitive man who lost his mate, became a community elder, had great care, compassion, and concern for the whole village and all life, died consciously in nature.

Past Life as Thomas

This story came to my mind in a 2+ hour long meditation which turned into a waking dream, or vision that I experienced one afternoon in the early to mid 2010's.

I laid down to meditate with an intention and desire to know about a past life. The desire was so deep and unshakeable that it felt like a prayer crying out from my soul. I asked the Universe to please show me a past life. This story came to me in that one afternoon's session, which lasted almost three hours for the body, but took me on a journey of several years.

This visionary, dream experience was as vivid as any waking, conscious experience I've ever had. And it remains so to this day. In the vision, I saw, heard, touched, tasted, smelled and emotionally "felt" sensations very clearly – just as clearly and completely as any waking, conscious experience sensed with the body and mind in the present, physical time and space.

I felt I was "awake" the whole time, but immersed in this other world, like a nighttime dream. After I came out of the meditation, I remembered every detail.

There was much more richness and detail in the vision than I am able to recount in this written version. As such, this written version is more of a sketch than a full retelling of the vision. But, I feel that is true of any retelling of any experience. When one tells a story of one's life, or single experience, or set of experiences, that telling can only be a summary sketch of the actual life, experience, or experiences and it is impossible to capture all the richness, detail and nuance. A classic example of this is the difference between eating an orange, or telling someone who has never done so what eating an orange is like. There is no way to capture and convey the actual experience of eating an orange by retelling it in words. That's how this telling of the story is – a summary description at best.

Given all the detail I experienced and remembered, I am convinced this is a life someone actually experienced. I "believe" it was my own past life. But, I don't "know" if it was "my own" past life, or another person's life. At this point, I don't think it matters. The important thing is that this is a life, or a metaphor of a dream, or a dream of a metaphor and I was given the gift of experiencing the essence, beauty, mystery, and lessons of this particular life experience now, in this lifetime, through my current conscious awareness.

Note: In this description, I have added comments *[in brackets with italics]* where I didn't see or experience details in the vision, but I had a "felt sense" of what happened. These bits are kind of like the reading or meaning between the lines of the literal scenes – they're in the background of the viewer's mind, but not directly, seen, heard, or felt in the vision. They are a more subtle aspect of the vision.

Comments About the Point of View and Pace of the Vision

I experienced most of this meditation or vision from the point of view of a boy who was 10 or 11 years old at the beginning and 15 to 17 years old toward the end. I call him Thomas, Tom, or Tommy.

Although most of the vision is from Tommy's perspective - as if I'm in his mind and body - the vision often shifted into the perspective of other characters' mind/bodies, or to a third person point of view as an "observer" in the scene seeing the overall picture unfold from a separate, invisible, passive viewer's perspective. I felt that this third person perspective was "camera-like" in its impassive, and impartial feeling tone. When the camera-like view happened, the experience felt less emotionally charged or opinionated. There was no value judgment even though there was often awareness of individual characters' thoughts, and feelings. The view was from the "outside" of the characters at those times, and it seemed as though that perspective was provided for additional breadth of understanding or fullness of experience of each "scene" or situation.

I'll also mention that some of these "scenes" played out slowly, as if they were unfolding at a "normal" pace, but then they would sometimes jump quickly to a time later in the day, or many days, weeks, or months later. And sometimes, instead of long, slow scenes, they'd flip by rapidly as if the pages of a book were flipping by. But, even when a sequence of scenes flashed through quickly, each "page", "snippet", or "glimpse" of a scene was there long enough for me to be aware of a richness of detail in the inner worlds of the characters, and it lingered long enough for me to be aware of the richness of the environment, or setting, when that was helpful or needed, (or if I was just "curious" and I wanted to pause and check it out to enjoy or notice).

Whenever the scenes "fast-forwarded", it seemed that they were shown that way to achieve an effect of linking, comparing, contrasting, transposing, juxtaposing, or resolving related pieces into a "thread". For example, a thought may happen one day, then a related one the next day, then a week later, then three months later, followed by a memory from years earlier, and then a related event a year later, and they would all be shown together in rapid succession to allow the mind to see and follow the pieces as one composite, connected "flow".

It's impossible to write all of this in the way it was shown. As I write it now, years later, I can't even remember all of it anymore. But, I have tried to write what I remember simply enough and yet catch enough of the highlights to give a sense of the overall arc and effect.

A Perfect Day

The vision started on a beautiful day with puffy clouds in the sky, sun shining, a light breeze, and perfect temperature. "I" am aware that this nice weather is unusual for this place. Most days the weather is overcast, windy, rainy or cold here.

[One thing I notice is that I have a question about who is the "I" that is experiencing all this in the dream? And who is the "I" that is observing? Are the dreamer and the person in the dream, the same person? Is it me, Mike, observing this, or is this another person's eyes, body, and mind I'm experiencing this through? It feels both "like me" and like it's another person and Mike is only an observer here, along for the ride through another person's consciousness. Hmmm, very interesting!]

Me [Tommy] and my sister, Mary, who is a year or two younger, stay pretty close to each other throughout the day and we stay close enough to our house to hear Nanna call if she wants us to come home early. Otherwise, we are allowed to stay out until dark. We have snacks wrapped in handkerchiefs, and our big dog is with us for fun and protection. It is a lazy day with no goal, no plan, and no purpose. The only thing to do is play, wander around, and daydream - an ideal day as far as I am concerned. The day is filled with wind in the hair, sun on the face, the smell of the salty sea breeze, and the beauty of sky, clouds, grass, trees, birds, and drowsy insects. Having Nanna nearby, lounging around with the dog, and talking with the sister (but only when I feel like it) is a perfect day and I know I'm lucky to have everything provided for me in such glorious abundance on a day like this. I don't have a worry in the world all day. Nanna doesn't call until the sun goes down. So, it's a full day of lounging and exploring. It is a day that resonates with a golden glow.

Tom and Mary

Tom is a smart, kind, and even-keeled kid. Even at his tender age of 11, he is somewhat philosophical about things. He is aware of a lot. He pays attention to things. He remembers and thinks about more things than most people. Tom notices other people don't pay attention and can't remember things the way he can and he wonders why that is. He feels lucky to be born the way he is - with such a good memory and such thoughtfulness even though he finds it a burden, at times, to remember everything and turn it over in his mind so much.

Tom realizes he is grateful for being grateful! He is grateful for his temperament. He doesn't have much. He thinks about having or doing "more", but he still feels lucky because it doesn't bother him too much. He's happy with what he has and he's not too upset when he doesn't get his way. His sister, on the other hand, is rarely satisfied. She is selfish and whiny and she usually wants something different than whatever she has. If she gets a candy, she wants two candies. If she gets a new dress, she wants different material, more colors, less colors, different pattern, more frills, less frills, or *something* different. Not only is she unhappy about something nearly all the time, she is quick to complain. She is adept at expressing her displeasure, and she doesn't hesitate to let others know when something bothers her. Tom notices he doesn't have the same problems she does in that regard. He is glad he isn't like her. Tom feels his way of being is mostly because he was born that way but also because it is a choice – to be grateful, positive, and pleasant.

[These aspects of Thomas' personality and character feel like the current "me", Mike.]

Life with Nanna

Tom appreciates his life with his Nanna (and even the sister) in their one room stone house by the patch of trees not far from the cliff on the edge of the ocean. He enjoys their dog, chickens, sheep, and cow. He LOVES his Nanny whom he and his sister Mary called "Nanna". He likes their little garden, the woods, and the big rolling, grassy fields around their house. He loves the inside of their little house too. On one side of the room is a big stone fireplace – almost tall enough to stand in. Close to the fireplace is the bed they all share – Tom, Nanna, and Mary. The rest of the room has a cozy corner where Nanna works on her sewing and cooking, and a table and chairs where they eat.

Nanna is the best. Out of everything in his life, Tom is probably most grateful for her. Living with Nanna and his sister, Tom thinks of Nanna as his example of how to be and his sister as an example of how not to be. Mary is bitter, sour, and generally unpleasant to be around, but he adores his Nanna. Tom doesn't know how old Nanna is. But she is "old" to him – maybe in her 40's or 50's. She is medium height and a little heavy set. She usually wears a scarf on her head, an ankle length skirt, a baggy, long-sleeve blouse, and an apron. Her facial features and outer appearance are not beautiful or even what most people would consider attractive, but to Thomas, her inner lightness, and her kindness, patience, and generosity make her the most beautiful person in the world.

Nanna always holds the kids first and foremost in her thoughts and actions. Everything she does is for them and with them in mind. When they have a bounty of food, or a few new goods they've traded, she always gives the best to Tommy and Mary (mostly Mary because she is needier). Nanna only takes for herself whatever is left over. This is true at every meal and in every sense with her time, her energies, and her emotions. Nanna serves Tom and Mary first and waits for them to have seconds and thirds until they are full before she eats. If there are good pieces of meat and some gristly pieces, Nanna takes the gristle. If there isn't enough meat in the stew for everyone, Nanna lets the kids have the meat, and she takes vegetables. If there aren't enough vegetables for everyone, Nanna lets the kids take the vegetables and she takes whatever broth is left. If it looks like there isn't enough food for the next day, Nanna lets the kids eat and she doesn't eat at all. Sometimes, Tom offers his food to Nanna, but she doesn't take it. At night, Nanna gets the kids comfortable and sleepy before she turns off the candles and lamps, and she stokes the fire one more time after the kids are asleep to keep it going through the night. In the morning, Nanna gets up early to start the fire and have the room warm and food and drink hot for Tom and Mary when they wake. She does everything like that – extremely thoughtfully, thoroughly, and with the utmost care and attention.

Sleeping next to Nanna at night is the most comforting, safe, and loving feeling imaginable. It's a true honor and blessing to have her as his Nanna.

Nanna works day and night for Tom and Mary. She works from before sunup, all day long, and until after sundown making, mending, and cleaning their clothes and bedding, cooking, tending the fire, and taking care of the livestock and garden. Nanna also spends a lot of time fixing Mary's hair and clothes, and talking with Tom, answering his questions, opening and guiding his young mind. Nanna is amazing!

Tom thinks of Nanna as his Mother, Nurse, Teacher, Angel, Saint, Provider, and Caretaker all in one.

The Contrast Between Nanna and Mary

Mary, in contrast with Nanna, is outwardly cute and pretty to look at. She has curly blondish brown hair, bright blue-green-yellow eyes and a pleasant, strawberry shaped face. But her attitude is horrible! The contrast and contradiction isn't lost on Tom. Nanna is plain, often dirty, and worn looking on the outside, but kind, gracious, gentle, loving, and giving inwardly and through her actions. Mary is just the opposite - pretty to look at but rotten at the core and with terrible behavior.

This gives Tom a sense that the inner self - character, and virtue - is more important and valuable than outer appearance, no matter how beautiful or superficially desirable the outer appearance of a person looks.

Visiting and Trading with the Neighbors

Once in a while they tie up the animals and leave the house to go visit neighbors. Some visits are social. Other trips are for trading supplies or securing services. The neighbors are a pretty far walk away. It seems to young Tom and Mary that it takes all day to get there and back. But, Tom enjoys it because he gets to see how other people live. It expands his world.

Nanna trades whatever they have for whatever they need. For example, Nanna trades eggs, vegetables, wool, sewing, or money for meat, flour, coffee, tea, sugar, cloth, rope, or help around the house.

The neighbors they visit most often are a kindly old couple who adore Mary and Tom. The lady, Alice, always has some little treat for Tom and Mary – a toy, or a snack. Alice dotes on Tom and always compliments his good looks, happy eyes, good manners, and calm, attentive demeanor. She is equally kind to Mary, complimentary of her inquisitive cleverness, and her hair and clothes. Unlike Alice, who naturally loves people and is animatedly expressive toward others, her husband, Mister Blake, is quiet and reserved. She expresses enough love of life and connection to others for both her and her husband combined. Mister Blake isn't sour or angry. He has a sense of contentment that shows through the twinkle in his eyes. But, he has no ability or need to talk with others about what he feels inside himself or what he sees or feels about others. He's kind of a silent, happy person. A person can feel his inner joy and satisfaction in his presence, but he's so guarded, one wonders exactly what's going on inside him.

The Blakes have a wagon and horses, so when Nanna, Tommy, and Mary need something from town, Nanna usually takes money to the Blakes and the Blakes pick it up in town on their next trip. The Blakes then take the goods to Nanna's house, or Nanna and the kids go get it from the Blakes the next time they visit.

Mrs. Blake – Alice – is Nanna's closest friend. Alice and Nanna enjoy each other's company and have a deep mutual respect for one another. Alice has enough joy and life for not only her and her husband, but also for Nanna. Nanna rarely laughs or even smiles when she is at home, but her eyes light up and she even smiles and laughs a little when they visit Alice and Mr. Blake.

Nanna has a deep, abiding satisfaction too – kind of like what one sensed in Mr. Blake. Her demeanor might best be described as a sense of fulfillment, purpose, or meaning with her life in the little stone house near the cliff by the woods with Tom and Mary, but she didn't seem happy. She seemed more like she was on a mission and she knew she was giving it her all and doing it very well. It was obvious she loved Tom and Mary abundantly. She showed affection, care, and concern for them. She hugged them and kissed them, and told them how wonderful they were, but she rarely used the word Love. She didn't say "I Love You", and she didn't show much joy either except when she was with Alice. Alice opened up her joy.

Tom, Nanna, and Mary sometimes visit a few other neighbors that are about as far away as the Blakes as well. But, these neighbors aren't friends. They are more like acquaintances. Nanna, Tom, and Mary visit them when Nanna wants specific goods or services. For example, one family raises animals and butchers them for meat. Nanna visits them to buy meat, usually lamb or sheep, but sometimes beef, goat, or poultry. Another man lives with his wife on their small farm and when Nanna needs repairs on her house or animal pens that she can't do herself, she trades with him or pays him to work at Nanna's.

Nanna provides a lot of what is needed from their own garden and livestock, but once in a while she judiciously takes coins out of a sack she hides in a wall (or maybe it is hidden in the fireplace). She gets coins whenever they need meat, repairs to the house, new clothes for the kids, or if Nanna feels they deserve a treat to celebrate. Celebrations are rare though – just a few times a year like in the Spring, after making it through another winter, or in Fall, after the harvest season but before another long, hard winter.

Tom and Mary's Father

Tom and Mary's Father is a merchant sailor. Tom and Mary understand that he owns a ship and that he organizes sea-going trade voyages where he takes cargo from his home port to distant places where he then unloads the transported cargo and then reloads the ship with new goods that he delivers to the next port or brings back home. He hires and manages crews of dozens of sailors and does business with merchants in distant ports. Between the sailing, trading, loading and unloading of the goods at all the ports, and the preparation of the crew and the ship between voyages, he's gone for months or even years at a time. The journeys are arduous and perilous enough that there is no telling if he'll complete any given voyage. Every time he leaves on a trip, it might be the last time Tom and Mary will ever see him. There are always tentative estimates about how long he'll be gone, but it is never certain.

The children rarely see their Father and when they do he is mostly thinking and talking about business. When he is home, he spends most of his time talking with Nanna about the household and the kids. He also talks about his future plans.

He leaves her with cloth sacks full of coins when he comes back from his voyages. No one knows how much he leaves with her. Some of the neighbors say it is just enough to keep his kids provisioned in his absence. Some think he has left a vast fortune with her. Whether it is a lot or a little, he does his best to leave enough for the children to be taken care of in his absence.

This is not something the Father or Nanna speak about directly with Tom and Mary. It is spoken in hushed tones between Father and Nanna and also maybe between Nanna and Alice. It seems that Nanna takes this responsibility of caring for the children and safeguarding the stash of money very seriously – like a sacred vow.

Young Tom doesn't know how all this works. The adults don't seem to want him to know, so Tom doesn't ask. But, Tom overhears just enough to get his interest and imagination going. Tom has a big imagination and he wonders about the arrangement between his Father and his Nanna. He fills in the gaps of what he knows for sure with his imagination.

Their father is a short, agile, muscular man. Most of the time, he has a stern expression. He is like a mythic figure. Even in his presence, he seems unreal. When he shows up at their house, he blows in like a storm, full of bluster, excitement, and exhaustion from the previous journey. He has sacks of gifts and loot from the trip. Then, after a few days or a week, he calms down and settles into the slow, tender domestic rhythm with Nanna and the children. His expression softens and he spends time, talks, and even plays with the kids. He lightens up, smiles, and even laughs some. But that only lasts a short while – a few days, to a couple of weeks, maximum. Then, just as suddenly as he bursts into the house, he begins to get worked up about needing to leave. The next big voyage becomes urgent and he starts talking about the need to get his crew together before they scatter. He also talks about the work the ship needs, and other preparations for the trip. He becomes concerned that he has to sail before the weather changes or the market for the next shipment passes, or something or other. He shifts toward a focus on the ship and the trades and he becomes detached from the household. Once he shifts into that state of mind, it gains momentum and he absolutely HAS to leave within a few days or a week, at the most.

He is hard, strong, resolute, energetic, and unyielding. His word is law. He is decisive and he has firm ideas about everything. He is a born leader.

It seems his life on the ocean is the life he is born to lead. The children and the situation with the Nanny don't match up well with his itinerant merchant sailing life. Yet, he clearly loves his children – fiercely even. He loves the challenges and camaraderie of the sea and his crew, and the power, respect, adventure, wealth, and commerce with his fellow traders. But, the children touch and fill a different dimension of him. His Love for his children is the deepest and most important aspect of his life. His family gives his life more meaning than anything else. But, ironically, it is also the one area of his life where he feels the least patient, competent, capable, and necessary.

Tom and Mary's Mother

The story Tom, Mary, and the neighbors heard was that Tom and Mary's Mother died several years earlier when the children were infants and their Father was on one of his voyages. Nanna was a domestic helper to the children's mother, and Nanna took care of the children and the affairs of the household after the Mother died suddenly. Then, when Father returned, he found that Nanna had done such an incredibly faithful and conscientious job that he decided to entrust the children to her in his absence from then on.

The story was that their mother came from a family of means, and the merchant Father came from a humbler background. When the Mother died, there was a falling out with the Mother's family. They blamed the Father for the Mother's illness and death. The Mother's parents wanted to raise the children, but the Father declined. The Mother's family had been significantly supporting the family while the Mother was alive, but after her death and the disagreement about the children, the Mother's family didn't provide as much financial contribution.

Father had concerns about finances and the children's wellbeing. Because of all these factors, Father decided to move Nanna and the children from their semi-affluent city dwelling to a modest, peasant property in the country. Father did not trust financial institutions, his domestic workers, or his in-laws. He wanted to keep his money and his children under his own control. He thought it would be too risky to leave them in the wealthy household in the city since it would pose temptations to the domestic workers, in-laws, and other scheming, city dwelling "friends" of the family. Another concern was the expense of keeping up a lavish household. That wasn't Father's style anyway. He wasn't interested in keeping up appearances. Father reasoned that moving the children into a modest and secluded arrangement with the Nanny would allow him to stretch his money farther, save more, and keep the money and the children secure. He thought it would be the best childhood for his kids and he hoped that by making this change he'd be able to save enough money after a few more journeys to settle down and live his later years with his children in relative peace and prosperity.

He moved the children to the country with the Nanny and entrusted his greatest treasures – his money and his children – to this humble, devout domestic servant for safekeeping until his return. This was a tremendous amount of trust - he trusted her with his life savings, and his children who were the most important people in the world to him, whom he loved with all his heart, and who he lived for.

It was a wise decision. Nanna was heroically hard-working and thrifty in her devotion to the children and the protection of his monetary assets.

Father and Nanna

When Father came home, Tom and Mary were not allowed to sleep in the same bed with Nanna and their Father. Their Father took their place in the bed. Tom also noticed that their Father and Nanna spoke in hushed and serious tones after they thought the children were asleep, or when the children were outside. Their conversations seemed to have great importance.

Father trusted Nanna. Nanna had a strength and depth of character that their Father leaned on and depended on just as much as the children did. One time when their Father was getting close to leaving, Tom saw their Father cry and he saw Nanna hold and console him. She had a warm and compassionate manner, and didn't seem to be as distraught as he was about whatever it was they were talking about. Tommy wondered if they were talking about Tommy and Mary's mother and how she passed away. Or maybe their Father was sad to leave Nanna and the kids. Tommy never knew. But he saw that even though their Father was so bold and had the courage and strength to put together his ship and manage the crews and sail around the world, he was still not as emotionally strong and solid and still and deep as Nanna. Their Father was like the wind and the Sea, but Nanna was like a rock or the Land or the Earth itself.

Father Leaves, Questions Grow

When their Father left, Thomas thought about him a lot. Thomas wondered if they really had another Mother, or if Nanna was their Mother. Nanna was so kind to them, so loving, so giving, and so proud of Tom and Mary that Tom couldn't imagine another Mother in her place. He started looking at her carefully for similarities to him and Mary. He couldn't really see any physical similarities, but she was old and worn now, maybe she looked different when she was younger. Maybe he'd look more like her when he got older...

Thomas had a BIG imagination and he began to formulate elaborate stories in his mind. He thought maybe his Father had Tom and Mary with Nanna but at the time she was a barmaid or a housekeeper and maybe Father had another wife. Or, maybe Father never married Nanna, and he had her live in the most remote possible place to keep his illegitimate children hidden. Maybe it was a strategy to protect another, legitimate marriage and family or business interest he had elsewhere. These thoughts went round and round in Tom's mind.

Tom had a *hunch* he and Mary were the illegitimate children of their Father and Nanna. He *felt* Nanna was their true Mother. But why would Nanna go along with the "Nanny" story if she was really their Mother? Maybe that was one of their Father's conditions for continued support. Maybe that was a story Father thought would keep them safe, so others wouldn't know they were the family of a wealthy merchant. Or maybe the man they thought was their Father was really their Grandfather, and Nanna was their Grandmother, and their real Father died at sea or in a war or something. Maybe their "Father" was just a kind stranger who was helping this woman and her kids out – whatever their parentage may have been. Or, how about this – what if the Father/Grandfather/Stranger was doing some difficult job to support the orphaned kids and their Nanny/Mother/Grandmother. Maybe the "father" was just a sailor, but not a wealthy ship-owning merchant and that's why he was gone so much of the time, and they lived in near-poverty conditions. Or, maybe "Father" and "Nanna" were really grandparents or adoptive parents and they told this story to protect the children from the harsh reality of their real parent's demise or apathy and neglect.

Also consider this: if their "Father" was so wealthy, why would he have his children live nearly destitute with a poor woman in the middle of nowhere and just a few coins to tide them over?

The story didn't add up to Tom. He thought some part of the story wasn't true but he didn't know which part. Maybe their Father wasn't their Father, or their Nanna wasn't their Nanny, or their Father wasn't wealthy and powerful, or something.

How is one to know what is true and not true, and should one even want to know?

Thomas didn't know how or why he thought of these things. He had never been exposed to such stories and intrigues. Come to think of it, Thomas couldn't remember if he had really even heard all these details about the story of his Mother before or if he had filled in the blanks himself. The whole story of his "Mother" dying when he and Mary were young and then Nanna and Mary and him moving to the country - he couldn't remember where all that first came from. Had he imagined that story too? How odd that Tom remembered most things but he couldn't remember the origin of this story.

For some reason, Thomas didn't feel this was something he could ask Nanna and expect to get an honest answer. But, he finally did ask, "Is that man really our Father, Nanna?" Nanna said "Yes". Thomas then asked Nanna if she was their Mother. Nanna didn't answer directly. Thomas detected some pain or sadness and he didn't want to cause her the least discomfort. So, he didn't ask again until he couldn't hold it in any more. He couldn't hold it very long, though. A few weeks later he asked again, and she avoided answering directly a second time. So, Thomas continued spinning theories.

He talked with Mary about these ideas, but Mary said he was being ridiculous. Mary said, "Nanna *is* our Nanny and not our

Mother. Our Mother died when we were little and Father is having Nanna take care of us and his money until he earns enough money to live with us for good. Don't question it Thomas. Why can't you believe it?"

Thomas couldn't shake his doubt, imagination, and curiosity about this. He didn't feel it was all true. His gut told him he was onto something with his doubt and questioning. He thought he was the only one beside Nanna and his Father who knew there was more to the story.

It was troublesome that he didn't know the full truth. But again, Thomas was so grateful, so fortunate, and so blessed with this lovely life with Nanna and a future of possibly following in his "Father's" footsteps as a great and powerful ship owner and wealthy merchant, that he thought it best not to question it any further for now. He thought the answer would unfold over time if it was supposed to, or remain a mystery forever if that was supposed to happen. He thought it would be best to hold off on these questions until he was old enough to work with his Father, and then he'd see the truth for himself firsthand. Also, he decided whether or not Nanna was his Mother didn't matter, in a way, because he knew she loved him like the best possible Mother, and he knew he would always provide for her and take care of her and be close to her as long as he lived. And he knew she would never abandon him and he would never abandon her.

Tom's Wanderlust and Problem with Mary

A few years passed without their Father. Thomas and Mary were growing older. Thomas was now about 15 or 16. Mary was a year or two younger. Thomas had become increasingly restless about his isolated, quiet life with Nanna and Mary out in the country. Once in a while he'd hear stories of adventure and experience from Mr. Blake or the neighbors. The stories made him feel he should go out into the world and experience more than was available to him there with Nanna and Mary.

Nanna let Tom have more freedom and independence. She'd let him go to the neighbors by himself. Once in a while, she even let him go to the cliff at the sea by himself. Tom loved it when he could go to that cliff, lie down on his belly, hang his head over the edge, listen, and watch the waves crash on the shore for hours. Nanna had seen Tom's natural curiosity and steady maturation over the years in diverse settings as she had exposed him to many people and places. She trusted Tom's innate character.

But, Nanna also sensed a growing restlessness that showed another side she hadn't seen in him before. She did her best to let herself open up to his need for broader horizons. She worried though, and she gave him profuse instructions on what to do and what not to do, when to come back, and so on, before each of his solo excursions. She let him go out on his own more and more but she had a hard time with it. It was harder for her than Tom. Tom was ready and he had no fear or worry at all, just excitement.

Another issue contributing to Tom's increasing restlessness was Mary. Mary was still selfish and annoying as ever. She became harder to tolerate as she got older, if that was even possible. Also, she started to blossom into a young woman and Tom felt uncomfortable around her. She was beautiful, actually, and Tom couldn't help sneaking glances at her and noticing the changes in her body. Just a few years earlier, when they were kids, they were not self-conscious about each other's bodies or different genders. If they had physical contact or saw each other's bodies, like when they slept in the same bed, bathed, swam, or played outside, it was no big deal. But now, Tom was getting more of a man's body and Mary was beginning to develop more of a woman's body, and it was awkward. He couldn't help himself. He couldn't control his urges to catch glimpses of the curve of her hips or developing breasts. And when they touched, he felt an excitement he didn't like. Sometimes he couldn't hide his physical reactions. He was repulsed by his sister but also excited by her. He needed to get away from her.

She knew she had this devilish effect on him and she played it to her advantage, using it against him to get what she wanted with Nanna too. She threatened to tell Nanna about him looking at her if he didn't do what she said. She made him promise not to go against her when she asked Nanna for anything. She would get undressed, walk, prance, and lounge around partially or scantily dressed to get Tom to notice her so she could use it against him, especially when she was preparing to throw one of her tantrums to demand something from Nanna. She played Tom to get control of him and get what she wanted from Nanna.

Tom kept himself under control. He didn't stare at her and mostly didn't even look at her in that way. He just found himself catching glances occasionally when he didn't keep himself in check. It was an unconscious reflex. He wasn't obsessed or tormented with Mary and he definitely wasn't obsessed with any sexual urges toward her. He was mostly repulsed and annoyed with Mary and her manipulations of him and Nanna, and also disappointed with his own impulses toward her. He decided he'd ignore her and his own urges as much as possible. It was confusing too, because he loved and cared about her as his sister, but found the sexual tension to be a hassle.

The annoying aspects of Mary, like the things she wanted didn't bother Tom that much sometimes because he just didn't care about what she cared about. Tom didn't care about Mary getting the fancy clothes or shoes. He didn't care about her getting so much of Nanna's attention for her hair, or her getting the best toys, best food, or any of that even though some of it was at his expense. He made do with whatever was available and he prided himself on needing as little as possible - just like Nanna and the opposite of Mary.

Tom didn't want to struggle with Mary's behavior or manipulations by counteracting them with his own. He didn't want to play her game. It wasn't important for him to make her "act right". He didn't think he could change Mary anyway, so he thought the best thing to do was let her have her way and her trivial concerns and petty behavior, but take a higher road himself which was truer to his character anyway.

Tom valued his daylong adventure trips, and he was glad to help Nanna around the farm and house with animals and chores. He valued those experiences and connections with Nanna more than having clothes or material things. He knew he liked experiences and adventure more than comfort and material possessions. His only possessions were a few changes of clothes, a small knife, boots, a hat, and some mementos he collected out in Nature – rocks, leaves, feathers, sticks, bones, and skulls. He was content with those things and his thoughts and imagination. He was happy to let Mary have the material and physical advantages as long as he could have freedom and the connections with Nature and Nanna.

As Tom got older, he began to pay attention to more things. When the neighbor came by to help fix the roof or work on the animal pens, Tom hung around, asked questions, and watched everything closely. He wanted to know how to do those kinds of repairs himself. When they bought meat, Tom asked if he could help slaughter the animals and prepare the meat. Nanna even let Thomas go by himself to the Blakes on occasion. Tom went with Mr. Blake to town a few times. Tom wanted to learn everything these neighbors knew so he could help Nanna and she wouldn't have to rely on others so much.

Tom learned as much as he could to see if that would be interesting enough to hold him there in the county and also to help Nanna, but he also sought to learn because he had an insatiable curiosity, and in a sense, a pull to grow up and experience the world. It could be called a *wanderlust*. He was pulled in two directions. On the one hand, he wanted to stay and help Nanna, but on the other hand, she seemed to have things under control, and he felt pulled to be with his Father.

Tom's imagination opened up widest when he thought about going to sea with his Father. Over time, Thomas becomes increasingly clear that he won't be satisfied with a life filled with nothing but taking care of the few animals, tending a small garden, and taking occasional longer trips. It is too small for him. Plus, Thomas is frustrated being around Mary.

Tom figures if he leaves for a year or two to learn about sailing and the merchant life, Nanna and Mary will be fine. He hopes when he comes back Mary might be more mature and less spoiled, or maybe she'll even be moved away by then. Tom becomes convinced he should follow his Father. He thinks Nanna will understand. He wants to see and learn what exists beyond his small sphere of experience so bad that he has to do it. It crowds everything else out of his mind. He reasons that after he is away for a while, he'll come back to Nanna anyway. He convinces himself he isn't abandoning her.

Dreaming of Life with Father

Tom wondered when or if his Father would come back. He asked Nanna if she knew anything. She said she never received advance notice before he returned. He just showed up unannounced. She said before he left last time he said it would be a long voyage and it might take a year or more before he'd be back. It had been over three years since he had last been home.

Tom wondered what it would be like to live on the ship with his Father and crew out on the sea. What did they eat and what kind of jobs did they do on the ship? Was it busy most of the time, or boring with lots of time to kill? Would it drive a person crazy to be stuck on the little ship with the same people for days, weeks, or months on end? Even if it was difficult, Tom thought he could handle it. He felt well prepared because it was similar to living in the close quarters of the little stone house with Nanna and Mary over the winters. Tom knew that living with Nanna and Mary afforded him a pretty big territory with the surrounding area in the woods, the sea, the neighbors, and town once in a while. That was a bigger territory than the decks of the ship and Nanna was giving him more freedom and responsibility all the time. But the ship was always moving, never static. The ship's territory was the whole ocean! And it must be a great adventure out on the water, going from place to place. And then, when the boat docks in a new port, the sailors get to go out on shore and explore the port towns. Even if they were confined to the ship most of the time, the water and the places they docked seemed like bigger horizons than the country life with Nanna and Mary.

Tom was ready to go out to sea from port to port with his Father.

Father Returns

Tom and Mary's Father returned to Nanna's house after maybe three and a half years. Father seemed much older, and less excited. It seemed like his life force was drained and the light and vigor around him was dimmed. Even his exhaustion was less pronounced, like he had to conserve energy to keep going and he couldn't let himself get too high or too low. He seemed worn down. His life and body seemed to be wearing thinner. There was less gleam and joy in Father's eyes, and not as much animation or expression in his talk or movement. The affection they felt from him so strongly on the last visit was much more subtle and subdued this time.

Thomas was brimming with excitement and energy about his decision to go with his Father. Thomas asked his father if he could go with him on the next trip, Father answers unequivocally, "No". Thomas cannot go with him.

Thomas wants to know why. He pleads his case. The answer is still no.

Thomas is sullen, then angry, then determined. This is his daydream and his night dream. He has a fever to go. He doesn't know when his Father will be back. Maybe never! Thomas feels he has to go NOW. He thinks this might be his last chance and he doesn't want to stay out in the country his whole life.

Tom Departs and Stows Away on the Ship

[There was no detail in this portion of the vision. But, I felt and "saw" something like an indistinct scene playing in another room, or behind a veil. It was like there was a stage play in progress right next to me, but I was behind the stage curtain, or in the next room. It was just outside my view and I couldn't quite hear or see it all. My body was getting restless and it felt like the

vision had to speed up before I went back into my body and normal consciousness.

I had a sense that Tom left the house, made it over to his "Father's" ship and somehow got on board. There were helpers along the way, but Tom deceived and manipulated them to get what he wanted. Tom felt a little guilty and concerned about Nanna and Mary. Nanna was beside herself with worry and guilt for not keeping him home.

At the ship, Tom hid in the cargo hold. He was discovered by a crewmember who helped him hide and kept him provisioned with food and water. This young man became his good friend and they spent time together and developed a bond. I call this man "Pablo" in the next scene.]

Darkness and Light, Out at Sea in a Storm, and Final Breath

[The scene is in the cargo hold of the ship. Thomas is there with the man who had been helping him stay hidden, "Pablo". Apparently, it was not safe, or a good idea for him to let his presence be known yet to his Father or the other men on the ship yet.

They've been at sea a few days already when the ship encounters a powerful storm.]

The ship starts bobbing up and down, then pitching and rolling from front to back and side to side. Then it starts twisting and slamming up and down. Men on deck are yelling and running around in a hurry. Animals in the cargo hold are agitated. Over the course of maybe an hour, the ship goes from rocking to getting tossed. The force of the storm becomes violent. A lamp is knocked over and it starts a small fire. Pablo and Thomas put it out quickly, but it is gets pretty serious. Pablo turns off all the candles and lamps to prevent another fire. The men from above deck open the hatch and yell something at Pablo. Thomas can't hear what they are saying because of the roar of the storm. It is raining hard – pouring. In the few seconds the hatch is open. A lot of water splashes into the cargo area. The ship seems like it is rolling almost all the way over to its side but it's hard to be sure which way is up. The sound of the rain and thunder is so loud Thomas can barely hear the donkeys and horses whinnying and braying right next to him. Thomas knows this is serious. He is scared.

The hatch opens again, and a lot more water pours in. Pablo climbs up the ladder to shut the door and the pouring water knocks him off the ladder and back onto the floor. The ship feels as though it is lifted up by a big hand and then slammed down on its side. The water keeps pouring in from the deck and this time the ship doesn't bob back upright. It stays leaning on its side. The animals slide to one side. Some of their ropes and chains break. Thomas climbs up on what used to be the wall which is now almost at the angle of the floor. Lightning flashes and in the flicker of light, Thomas sees the fear in the animals' eyes. Men from the deck are yelling to Pablo. Pablo is still trying to get over to that door, but he is also calling for Thomas. In a matter of what seemed like a few seconds, certainly no more than a minute or two, the cargo area is beginning to flood with saltwater. Thomas is trapped on the opposite side of the cargo hold from Pablo. There are so many boxes tossed around and hay floating in and on top of the water, plus animals kicking and yelling, Thomas can't quite tell where Pablo is or which way is up or out.

Thomas sees the water level rising and he knows he better make a move toward Pablo. He hears Pablo yell, and a moment later, he decides to let go and swim in the direction where he heard Pablo yell. As he swims out into middle of the upside-down, sideways cargo space he sees something right in front of him in a lightning flash. It is Pablo. He is underwater. His eyes are open and it looks like he is reaching out toward Thomas. Thomas and Pablo are both being tossed around. Thomas can't tell if Pablo was swimming or floating, under the water. He might have even been dead when Thomas saw him.

Thomas dives underwater and swims toward Pablo. But it is dark and he can't find him. Thomas holds his breath as long as he can, then swims up to the surface. It is interesting how Thomas still knows which way is up even though the water is thrashing and swirling so bad. Thomas takes a big breath and tries again. There's another lightning flash. Pablo is nowhere to be seen. Pablo has probably drowned. Thomas has to try to save himself. Thomas knows where he is in the cargo bay. He is toward the nose of the ship and the cargo hatch door is farther back toward the middle of the ship. The nose of the ship is pointing up and the hatch door is underwater. The water level is rising fast. Thomas has to make a strong push for the cargo door, or he'll be trapped inside and he'll drown too. Thomas takes as big a breath as he can and swims toward the door. He swims hard but he knows he will need a breath soon. He isn't sure whether to push harder and hold his breath a little longer – longer than he thinks he can - just in case he is close to the cargo door. But, he thinks, if this cargo hold is underwater, I'll still be underwater when I go through the door, so I'll need to save enough air to make it back to the surface from the other side of the door. Thomas decides to go back to the air pocket at the nose of the ship inside the top of the cargo hold. He tries to relax and swim with less effort to conserve his oxygen. He feels his way along some edge of the ship inside the cargo space and pulls himself along it to go "up" to the air pocket. His lungs feel as though they are going to burst. He lets all his air out slowly and he can't go any longer. He needs to breathe in, and just then, his head pops out of the water into a little pocket of air about one or two feet from the top inside corner of the ship. Thomas gasps to recover from the oxygen deficit, his lungs and muscles are burning and exhausted yet feel extra alive. Two feet of air space quickly becomes 18 inches and this is it. Thomas knows this is his one last chance to swim to the cargo door and get to the surface of the open ocean in the middle of the storm. He breathes several big breaths, then an extra big one and he dives in, remaining surprisingly calm and focused. He swims hard but can't tell if he is going in the right direction. He bumps on a side of the ship and tries to feel if it is a corner by the deck. He can't tell. He lets loose and swims in the water since his progress is too slow trying to feel and pull his way around the edge. There is another lightning flash and Thomas sees the door. He also sees Pablo floating underwater. They were far away from each other. Thomas swims toward the door. Involuntarily, Thomas takes a big inward breath – of water.

He feels his lungs burn and he is coughing but it is all underwater. He can't stop his body now. It breathes in and out but it is breathing water instead of air. He's still trying to swim and float to the surface but his body has no power. The body doesn't obey his commands to move. His eyes seem to let more light in and it is as though he can see in the dark. Is there more lightning now? Why can he see everything? There is no sound - just a beautiful silence. Thomas sees a beautiful light shining through the water towards him. It looks like rays of the sun pouring through trees in a forest on a misty day but through the water instead. Pablo is right there over toward the light – smiling and happy as if he has something to tell Thomas.

Thomas feels a panic and anguish. Is he dead? Had those breaths of water been his last? Surprisingly though, Thomas also feels an incredible warmth, weightlessness, peace, calm, love, belonging, and beauty. The positive feelings are far stronger than the fear, anger, and frustration.

He thinks of Nanna. His heart and soul call out to her. Will she be OK? In that flash of beautiful warm, golden, blue, green, turquoise light, he knows Nanna is OK. He knows she will be OK in the future, and he knows she will forgive him and always love him just as he always loves her.

Lessons and Messages from The Life of Thomas

The main lessons from this lifetime are recurring themes for me.

1. I have a desire for adventure – to experience something out there that will make me more complete.
2. This sense of adventure can become obsessive and take me out of balance.
3. I have a calm, quiet, observing, caring, and kind nature.
4. I sometimes have unhealthy fixations on the opposite sex that I attempt to actively manage and keep in check.
5. I saw Nanna as heroic because of her innate qualities and character. I wanted to emulate Nanna's good qualities to the best of my ability.
6. I saw the sister and Father as flawed characters because of their selfish desires and behavior. I felt those attributes were examples of qualities to avoid.
7. My deepest core value had to do with my Love for Nanna and a desire to reciprocate her kindness and giving of herself to others.
8. I regretted leaving her, but I knew all was forgiven, despite the emotional upheaval and even pain.

9. I was at my best when it was quiet and I could reflect and dream. But, there was a healthy, and even inevitable balance between calm, resting life, on the one hand, and turbulent, striving and seeking for more, on the other.

Life Between Lives

Sometime after I had the Life of Thomas meditation experience, a friend told me about Michael Newton's books, and I read them. Then, I felt drawn to have an LBL session myself.

In October, 2015 I went through a hypnotherapy process called Life Between Lives. The process guides a person into aspects of their own consciousness that are below (or beyond?) normal, ordinary, waking consciousness. There are no "suggestions" planted in the client's mind by the hypnotherapist. It's more like a guided meditation designed to help the client get into a deeply calm state of open awareness. It starts with a specific sequence designed to take a person back through their current life, then into a past life, and finally, into the time "between lives". The premise is that this time "between lives" is a time and place of profound peace, beauty, rest, and harmony that is by design restorative and integrative, allowing for review of the past life and preparation and choice of the future life. Through thousands of case studies, it has been reported that people have found great peace and healing by remembering their experiences as souls in their life between lives.

The process was developed by Michael Newton, PhD and is described in his books Journey of Souls: Case Studies of Life Between Lives (1994), Destiny of Souls: New Case Studies of Life Between Lives (2000), and Life Between Lives Hypnotherapy (2004) which are all based on sessions he conducted with clients. Another book in the series entitled Memories of the Afterlife (2009) was released later based on sessions facilitated by other therapists, but selected and edited by Michael Newton. Michael Newton passed over into life between his lives in 2016, and now, another case study compilation is in the works. It will be the first posthumous book in Michael Newton's oeuvre. My LBL session that I include here has been selected for inclusion in that volume. It is tentatively titled Wisdom of Souls and scheduled to be released soon, possibly in 2019. I will be called "Marc" in that book and it will probably be an edited version of what's included here. We'll see...

This LBL session was an important event on part of a bigger journey for me. It was amazing! It opened up my life. It was healing and it expanded my resilience and patience with myself and others. It's still active and alive in me as I live this lifetime on a journey as a soul.

The LBL process and a portion of my regression

The LBL process involves multiple steps. The first step is to prepare for the session by identifying significant people from one's past and listing questions one wants to ask during one's life between lives. Then, there are (at least) two hypnotherapy sessions. The first is a past life regression, and the second is the life between lives session.

The Past Life regression is covered in the next chapter of this book (Past Life as Chokrel). But here, I'll explain the LBL session.

First, the hypnotherapist and the client meet and greet. The therapist offers the client a comfortable posture. In our case, I accepted my therapists offer for me to sit in a big, comfy recliner covered with a light blanket. Next, the therapist goes through a series of calming and relaxing visualization and counting processes. These are like "guided meditations" that I've experienced in other settings where another person is talking, but I am having my own experience around the words that are being spoken. The best guided meditations have an openness that allow those involved to experience their own thing, not just what is being talked about. This guided meditation fit the bill of "best" for me, and I fell right into deep relaxation and visualization.

After the general calming and relaxing portion of the session, it moved into a portion where I moved backward in time through my own, current life. In this portion, the therapist stopped me at a couple of different ages approaching birth, to explore snippets of experience during those times in more detail. I was stopped at two ages, I think maybe around 17 and 7. I was asked specific questions about my life at those ages. I remembered some obscure facts that I hadn't thought about in a long time. One of the questions or suggestions for age 7 was to recall a pleasant, positive experience. The memory that came to me was my brothers and I splashing in a kiddie pool in our backyard. Our Mom was with us and it was a wonderful, fun moment, with no concerns or worries, and everything happy and good in the world at that moment. Even the recollection of that memory was deeply healing for me.

That was part of the prep for going between lives.

Next, the regression continued to birth, then into gestation in the womb where there were more questions about how I felt in utero and when my soul entered the body. I found all this fascinating. The recall of all this popped into my mind easily but my ordinary, logic, and ego-based mind was still active and it questioned all this. "Was it real? Where did all this come from? Was it just my imagination?"

But, it was so peaceful, comfortable, and pleasant that the judging, rational mind was able to "let go" of its skepticism at that moment and treat all this "as if" it was "true" for the moment. Anyway, it was very interesting and even exciting, so I wanted to continue and allow this other aspect of awareness, consciousness, or memory to unfold. I didn't want to fight it with judgment and skepticism.

After the time in utero, we went into a past life. In particular a past life that was selected by my companion "guide" in the session. This past life was a life that had a special lesson or gift for me.

LBL past life as Amara and her ceremony by the sea

The transcript below was done by the hypnotherapist who worked with me on my LBL session in preparation for submission to the Newton Institute for inclusion in Wisdom of Souls. The book's not out yet, so it may be edited even further. In the book my name is changed to "Marc" to protect my identity. But, I'm identifying myself as Marc and identifying this as my session to "unprotect" myself.

Notes:
1. The therapist lightly edited the actual words spoken during the session for brevity.
2. *She added her observations and comments in italic.*
3. *[I added my comments to her transcript in square brackets and italic].*
4. SML is the therapist and M is me, Mike.

~~~~~~~~~~~~~~~~~~~~

SML comment: For this LBL session I guide Mike to a past life through usual relaxation and guided imagery procedures. We begin our dialogue immediately following my suggestion that he go to a "different time and different place."

SML: Look down at your feet and scan up your body and tell me what you are aware of.

M: I have white cloth on my feet.

SML: Do you have a sense of whether you are inside or outside?

M: I hear the sound of water and waves. I'm in a cave by the ocean.

SML: Do you feel like you're a male or a female?

M: I'm a female.

SML: How old are you?

M: I'm in my early 30s.

[I was wearing a loose-fitting, flowing, white gown.]

SML: So tell me what's going on right now ... What is important to know about who you are, and where you are, and what's going on right now?

M: It's a worship ceremony having to do with the sunrise.

[I didn't verbalize it, because I was so astounded. But, in the regression, I was utterly amazed at this setting with the waves gently breaking against the sand and rocks in this dark, damp, womblike amphitheater / cove. The temperature and breeze were perfect – so powerful, yet comfortable and soothing. The time was right before sunrise.]

SML: Are you alone, or are others with you?

M: There are others with me. They're kind of hunkered down around the edge of the space. They are part of the ceremony too, but I am leading the ceremony.

[I was so dazzled by the beauty and power of this setting and what happened with the first rays of the sun that, at first, I didn't realize anyone else was there. I was pretty full of myself and proud of myself for having "conjured" all this. I was so caught up in myself and the phenomena, that I wasn't aware of the others. It was only when the therapist asked if there were others that I realized there were.]

SML: Are the others with you male or female?

M: They're all females.

SML: Tell me more about the ceremony and what happens next.

M: I have the sensation of pure pure light. I'm a spirit and there's another spirit there with me……. it's like an experiment.

[We were waiting for the first light of the sun. When the sun crested over the horizon, I felt and saw a ray of light travel all the way from the sun to Earth's horizon. Then, in a continuation of the same flash, the "ray", or ball of light, continued all the way to the cove with us. A ball of light shot from the sun and crossed the earth at light speed. Then, it came to a complete stop and stayed alive and resting with us in the back of the cove, right next to me. Since this happened at the speed of light, I was amazed that I had been able to see it travel across that distance. It was like I had a super-slow-motion perception to be able to see this particle or mass of light move through space as it traveled. Then, when the spirit came to rest, I felt its incredible power and its loving and giving consciousness.]

SML: Do you get a sense of the energy of that spirit?

M: The spirit has tremendous energy.

[She was like a 10 Gigawatt fairy godmother or guardian angel.]

SML: And what is the relationship between you and this spirit?

M: I feel it's a kindred spirit, and the spirit has joined with me.

[It's strange that I said that, because I also felt, in that flash, and her presence next to me, that she was not personal in scope. She was not my personal guardian angel. She was much grander than that. She was like a goddess angel, or something. Maybe she was a goddess of light?]

SML: Can you get a sense of the purpose of the ceremony?

M: My sense is that the purpose of the ceremony is a deep honoring of our origins or something like that - our beliefs and practices.

SML: Is there any more you can tell me about yourself and your role in the ceremony?

[The spirit was showing me that she is an example of who we all are. All of us are made from this same capacity and power, and we are indeed that. I was both so dazzled, and floored at the experience, that in attempting to answer the question, all I could feebly come up with was the following reply...]

M: I am starting to sense that I am a guardian spirit in the ceremony.

[A more accurate description would be to say that the other guardian spirit and "I" become one in this ceremony, and the merged "we" were exalted as one. The purpose is not to pump up the ego of the individual person, me, in the ceremony, but rather, it is an example of this principle in any and all of us.]

SML: What else can you tell me about yourself in that same lifetime?

M: Earlier, before going to the ceremony, I was just a woman in my community.

SML: What is your name? What do they call you?

M: My name is Aria .... or Ariala,

SML: What is your role in the community?

M: My role is like a healer and teacher and a helper of the community.

SML: Can you get a sense of the place you are in and the time in history?

M: I'm getting that it is in England. About 1,000 years ago.

SML: What else you can tell me? Anything else that is significant to know about that lifetime?

M: It's interesting that I don't sense many males around ...... there are some, but mostly females. It's a matriarchal society, and the women guide the community. They have the knowledge and are very connected with nature and each other. It's not about power. It's a very harmonious existence working for each other's mutual benefit.

SML: How do feel about this lifetime?

M: I'm very pleased with this lifetime, very happy.

Ariala's death

SML: So now we are going to move forward to the very last day of that life as Ariala.

I suggest with some emphasis: Be there now .... it's the Last day of that lifetime.

And tell me, is there anything going on that suggests this will be your last day?

M: Early in the day I have no sense that this is going to be the last day of this lifetime.

SML: And how old are you on this last day?

M: I'm not very old.

SML: So move forward and tell me where you are and if the setting is familiar. And tell me what is happening as the day goes on.

M: We are setting out on a journey to go somewhere. It may be on my way to the ocean, but I'm in a dark place like in the woods, and I'm sensing a lot of dread. I just see darkness, like something's being hidden from me.

SML: What happens next?

M: We're being attacked.

SML: Just detach from the body and float over the scene as if you're an interested observer, and from that perspective, just tell me what happens.

M: Ariala was going along the trail with a couple of female companions, and some men jumped out and attacked them. Ariala was trying to talk to them calmly and appeal to their sense of reason, their higher aspect, but it didn't help. They stabbed these women and maybe raped them. They stole what the women had, which wasn't much.

SML: From your perspective, floating above the scene as an observer, tell me what happens to you.

M: My spirit rises and detaches. I'm floating above the body.

SML: As you move away from your physical body, you'll be able to talk to me and answer my questions. Now you are in touch with your inner self and feel your mind expand to the highest level of your being. All physical pain and discomfort is left behind, and as you look down at your body you may perceive some sadness.... tell me where you find yourself in relation to your body.

M: I'm floating about 50-100 feet above the body.

SML: Is there anyone still near your body at this time?

M: Those thieves and murderers are still there around my body.

SML: So tell me how you're feeling right now.

M: I'm mostly angry and shocked that people could be like this. The community we lived in was a spiritual community, and we were shielded from this kind of behavior and aspect of the human condition. This was a big shock. I thought I would be able to communicate with them. I had my whole life ahead of me, and I feel like it was way too soon for this life to be over. I feel a little sad but more angry and shocked. I feel compassion too. I feel a lot of emotions because it happened so suddenly.

Client leaves the body behind and begins to leave the earth plane.

In Between Lives

SML: As we move on you'll be able to remember many details about your journey back home.

As you move upward to the loving realm of an all-knowing power, everything will become very familiar to you. As you move away from your body in perfect comfort, you will be returning home. And as we move away from your body, tell me everything that happens.

M: I meet that being again...the one that was in the cave. And it's a powerful and peaceful being. I realize that it doesn't have a gender, it's really just light energy and WOW(!), It's an amazing being. When it was with me for the ceremony, it presented itself to me before like a human being, but it's really just energy, and I'm energy, too, at this point, and this spirit is moving with me.

SML: You're moving together?

M: Yes.

SML: Can you give me more detail about the sense of this entity and if it is familiar to you?

M: Yes, the entity is familiar to me.... this entity is always with me. I asked it, and it told me yes.

SML: What else can this entity tell you about your connection?

M: It can tell me anything and everything. I'm just enjoying being with him.

SML: So just take a moment to do that, and when you're ready you can tell me a little bit more. Just tell me what you're doing.

M: Every time I leave the body I enjoy being with his energy. Now we are traveling ... we are traveling a great distance across space, and it's so much fun. It's just a big adventure, and it's fun! I love this ... we're laughing.

SML: So you've done this many times before?

M: Yeah. We have done this many times before.

SML: How do things appear to you?

M: At first it looked like a whole galaxy, and now it looks like an amorphous light that extends out for a way, not as big as a galaxy, but more like a big city or something.

SML: As you keep moving, tell me what happens next.

M: There is energy. It's the same as the being (entity). It's the same as me. It can appear or present itself into a humanly recognizable configuration, but it does not need to do that.

SML: When it does do that, how does it appear?

M: It's really cool. It's like it's more than three dimensional ... like spokes going on to a wheel into a hub and the spokes are going in all directions. It's like amorphous energy but with denser energy that is more concentrated towards the middle. It's not all going to one hub. There are several little pods.

SML: So where do you go next?

M: We are going toward the middle part of it, but I know that we're just going to go out to another spoke, or pod. It's beautiful colors like orange, magenta, light purple and yellow. It's really beautiful, and the pods are like little spheres. I'm dazzled by the whole configuration. It's really cool.

SML: Is there a set way that you like to go?

M: Yeah, it feels familiar ... I am going down certain corridors. I'm going down a corridor, and I know I'm going to be turning right. Now I'm in the middle of a whole configuration. It's like a huge cavernous room almost. There's a lot of stuff there. It's like Grand Central Station, but much grander. It's orderly, and there is a lot activity and everyone is excited about going to their places.

SML: So it's sort of like a terminal?

M: Yes, it's like a terminal, and they are all headed into different places and people are with their entities, like guides and they're saying things like, "Am I really supposed to go down this hall?" and their guides are saying, "Yeah, that's it." And they're looking at boards, kind of like message boards, and other people are just going on their own in a hurry. I'm anxious to be going down my hallway. I know where I'm going.

SML: Is the entity with you guiding you?

M: Yeah. The entity with me is a guide for me. This being is so wonderful, both male and female energy, strong, loving, patient and also gently forceful.

SML: Do you know your guide's name?

M: I will ask..... The name is Asriel, or something like that, but I think maybe that's just a joke.

SML: So just move on down your hallway and just describe to me where you are going and how it appears to you ... you've been this way before...

M: Yeah, it's so exciting ... I'm going down what looks like a long circular, cylindrical kind of shape and a lot of shapes branching off into pods, and maybe it goes out beyond and there are a lot more that branch out more and more. They funnel into like ... collector hallways. I don't know how many layers there are, but people are going down all the different ones.

In Between Lives with the Guide and Soul Group

SML: So follow along where you are going and tell me where you go.

M: When I arrive at where I'm going it is like a big surprise party. I know there's going to be a party...I can feel their excitement and my excitement. I'm going in to that big area and there are maybe 12 or 20 beings in there.

SML: Are these beings familiar to you?

M: Yeah they are all familiar to me. There is so much happiness there. It is more just like twinkling light.... just energy. I'm not getting language...they're happy. Two or three came forward initially and greeted me. Now I am just enjoying feeling their energy. The three that came forward are very familiar to me. It is interesting that when I went in there I noticed that there were some entities in there that were not altogether positive. I was surprised about that because I was looking forward to it and anticipating it so much and feeling so much positive energy about going there, but there were some that I get the sense were kind of sneaky. Maybe it's just part of lifetime patterns, but I still felt that. The three I'm with are very harmonious, supportive and compatible. These three are so loving, gentle, and kind. I'm trying to figure out who they might be in this lifetime.

SML: Ask them to reveal themselves to you.

M: One is my friend, Mary, and one is Flora. The other is my friend, Chittak.

SML: Perhaps you can ask them to tell you about the sneaky ones.

M: (Laughs) I'm skittish about knowing about the sneaky ones, most of them are not sneaky.

There are about ten others or so that are wonderful....all of them are wonderful, but some of them just agreed to take on these difficult roles. That's part of it........that is how they do it.

SML: Is that a pattern with your group, and is it usually those same entities that take on those roles?

M: I guess so, yeah. Some of them seem to enjoy it. That's what bugs me! (Laughs)

SML: Does that serve a purpose to the group as a whole?

M: Yeah it does. We are a group that are of service to others. We are caretakers, and we care about others. I do not get the sense that we have that many heroic, large-scale endeavors. We do significant things, but it's on a smaller scale. We love humans on earth. We create peace on earth and love wherever we are in whatever communities or families we are in, and when we do it, we are creating energy that moves out throughout the world. But we do it on a small scale with small groups. We have different configurations of people from the group that come together in different lifetimes.

SML: Have any of the ones that you consider to be sneaky been with you in physical lifetimes for certain reasons?

M: Yeah. A lot of the sneaky ones have been in lives with me.

SML: What roles have they played, and what roles have you played?

M: One of them was my murderer in that last lifetime. It makes me mad, but I know there is a purpose. I have a feeling that my dad and my brother in my current life have been challenging to me, but not in a really harsh way. *[They're part of this soul group.]* Others have shown me different ways of being so that I can have the experience.

So sometimes they have roles like that, that are not quite as exalted as I think I am. I'm kind of arrogant. In some lives they show me my arrogance, and I have to work on that. We all agree to do different things each time. Like our son, Carlos, is in this group. I think he's more of a playful spirit, and he doesn't ... I don't get the sense he is trying to do evil stuff, but it's very unconventional. He is more of a playful spirit, and he breaks all the rules in the roles, but he's playful like a jester. That's the way he gives others in the group perspective that the cultural norms are too small. He plays with it, and he knows he is violating the rules. He takes on some roles that are difficult.

SML: Are you getting any messages from the group about the life you just lived?

M: It's such a party, and everyone's happy to see each other, so it's not very organized. They are telling me that I did a lot of what I was supposed to do in the life as Ariala to help others understand the connection to our origins, our spirits and the peace that is within us. I did that very well, but, as usual for me, I was a little too serious. I could have lightened up. I was very focused and on task. I was a driving force in that spiritual community, and I was effective. But I could have had more fun with it. I healed many generations with what I did, but I still need to learn to lighten up and ... that's what it is ... in a way it was time for me to get out of that life because I wasn't really getting it, and it was time for me to exit that life because I was starting to get a little too caught up in the power of my position. I was connected in one way, but I was not getting it. There is a greater purpose to life and death, and the way it unfolded as well. One, or maybe both, of the other girls that were with me, survived and were able to deliver that message back to the community, and the community learned to be a little more careful, as it can be dangerous. I was feeling pretty invulnerable, and I went right up to these guys with knives and talked to them and told them it was wrong to do this, and it did not work. I was too direct, and I wasn't tuned into others enough. The surviving two girls conveyed that to the others and that was incorporated into their practices, and they were safer as a result. They understood more of the reality of things beyond them as they were very isolated.

SML: So two purposes, one that you were not making enough progress and at the same time you helped your village. What more can they tell you that is important to know about that lifetime?

M: They said it was so good that we practiced following our intuition and we deeply believed and practiced what we felt intuitively. Even though we did not have many teachers, we understood, and we were really worshiping what we felt, which was the sun, the ocean, nature, as we felt deeply that what we had was the origin of our human selves as well. It was really cool that we understood as much as we did and worshipped the way we did, and it's similar to what we have done over and over again. They are telling me about connections in terms of community to the same principles and ideas, but there are patterns of isolation and then connection in terms of community with other human beings, and that's just how it has to go. We keep learning the same thing in all these communities, and it's connecting back to the same thing about our origins and the peace within, and what we experience in this little pod here is that we're energy, and we don't harm or hurt each other. We need to experience that in the physical, such as in this last life.

SML: Do you work with any other groups too?

M: Yeah.

SML: And what is the purpose of that?

M: We work with other groups. I'm not sure about the purpose, but the way it works is the same as within our own small group, but maybe extended out to 10 or 12 other groups. So sometimes we work with other sister groups that are closely connected groups to incarnate in lives for certain lessons. So there is cross coupling and cross sharing, but they are more in outer circles.

SML: So while you are still with your group is there anything more that is important to communicate before we move on to our next stop?

M: The main communication is just love.

In Between Lives with the Guide and Council

SML: So now ask Asriel if it may be time to move on.

M: He says it is time to go to the Council.

SML: Tell me how you get there.

M: (*with a changed tone*) Oh. Things have become a little more serious now, and we're moving out of the pod area through the series of hallways in reverse order of how we came there, going back towards the central hub area, and it is like we are going to another, like pod-type thing. A sphere, but it is closer to the central hub. It looks like it's another little tunnel, but it is like a conference room.

SML: How does the conference room appear to you?

M: I feel like there are doors. It's kind of closed. We have to go through doors so we can get into it from the main central area. It's like an inverted V shape. Like on a bench but more like an inverted V pointing up.

SML: How many elders do you see?

M: There are nine, and four are on either side of the V and one is in the center. I stand in front of them. They are just energy so they don't need to stand or sit.

SML: How do they appear to you?

M: They appear to me as..... at first I saw them with features, I don't know why, but I was feeling a defensiveness, but then I allowed myself to really feel them, and there is no judgment at all. It's not a judgment like a courtroom. Not like a council where they're going to approve your zoning.

SML: What message do they communicate to you?

M: I'm really afraid, and I'm looking back at my guide saying, "What's going on?" Now his name becomes more like Orion rather than Asriel. Before, there was a playful quality, and now it's getting really serious. Orion is telling me it's okay, and I feel like a scolded kid. He's telling me to pay attention and it's okay. *[Orion is reassuring me and giving me a felling I'm not being judged and I won't be punished.]*

SML: What message are you receiving from them?

M: They are very patient with my fidgeting and resistance and all that, and they're telling me that you can't force others to do what you think or what you know is best for them. It is their choice. They are telling me about patience ...... I still need to learn a lot of patience. My impulses and my instincts are good and so receptive to good things, but I need to be more accepting of others and their choices. I have to learn that, and when I have learned that I'll be much more effective with my involvement in my teaching and guidance or whatever it is I'm doing.

SML: What advice can they give you about how you can best to do that?

M: They are saying, "Lighten up," and they're all laughing and really bouncing around.

SML: Do you have a habit of being too serious?

M: Yes. I'm embarrassed like a little kid.

SML: What else do they have to say?

M: They tell me they're always available to me, and I can visit them with Orion/Asriel at any time. And I would do well to remember this moment and the feeling of their patience and their love for me. They are not saying it that way, but I'm saying it that way, and that we are all guides for each other. We are all spirits for each other, and that's the main thing. I feel their love and support and kindness, and if I do that I will be fine.

SML: Would it be appropriate now to ask one of your questions?

M: Yes.

SML: Your first question is: What do I need to be shown, or what do I need to know right now at this point in my soul's journey for my current life as Mike?

M: They tell me I should just work with Orion on that, and that it's not a council question.

SML: Let's see about your other questions. Your next question is: What is my soul's purpose? What can I do to better align with that purpose?

M: They say that Orion, my guide, can spend more time with me on that, so I'm just tuned into one guide, and I'm not on the defensive and feeling like a little kid since we are more like pals. Here I feel intimidated even though there's no reason to feel that way.

SML: So we can save your questions for later when you can do that, but while we're still there, what else do they feel is important for you to know, or is there anything you would like to ask them?

M: They are telling me they appreciate me, and I am on the right path and doing the same work with a higher purpose. The Council is really giving...... like accolades: recognition and appreciation ....that this is who I am and what I do and have done, lifetime after lifetime for a really long time. They say to keep it up and keep the channel open to receive messages and guidance from them. Trust it because it is subtle when you are in a body, but trust it, and believe it, and know it, and sense this connection with the Council is always open. It flashes in and out, but I can ask for it, I can request it, and then I can receive the encouragement anytime and the guidance too.

SML: What do they say is the best way for you to access this as easily as you can?

M: They say to just get quiet and ask and open up to that guidance and listen. They say just carry on, it's okay.

SML: So what are your feelings about yourself now the meeting is drawing to a close?

M: They're not in that V shape anymore. That was so I would take them seriously. Now they're more surrounding us ... me and my guide. They appear luminous, and they are surrounding us.

Wow, this is so beautiful, it's beyond any words. Really, they are just letting me feel the appreciation and unity, and it's beyond anything I can convey in words. It's like they're charging me up .... helping me to trust the feeling of being charged up.. It's like everything went away except for them and the energy going through them. My guide is so supportive, and they are channeling a tremendous amount of energy.

SML: Do you get the feeling that there is a "higher" entity present at this meeting?

M: Yes, there is an overarching higher being that is included in all of it, and I can feel that. The Council members are like an example of the overall energy. That is an amazing feeling. They say just feel that, be that. Trust it.

SML: You always can.

M: I had all this self-doubt like I was going in to be punished ....like, "Am I doing the right thing?" They're showing me to feel the goodness and let it flow from the inside out. There is no time.....it's not just like "class dismissed" when I leave the chamber.... When you experience it, it continues forever. (*After a pause*) Wow! Now it's like I am exiting through a different dimension. It's like I came in horizontally, and I'm going out vertically. Up and down.

Wow! I'm exiting with my guide now.

In Between Lives with the Guide and Diamond Buddha

SML: Where do you find yourself now?

M: So now it's "me and the guide time."

SML: Where do you go?

M: We go wherever we want. It felt like we were in the middle of outer space or something, but we can create whatever environment we want to be in for our time together.

SML: So what do you create?

M: Well, I'm happy just in space, but, wow, I mean, I can just barely have the hint of an idea of a nature scene or tropical rain forest with a waterfall, and it instantly happens. I'm like a kid in a candy store. Is that what I really want? This is awesome. I'll just pick one thing, it'll be ok. I'll just go with that one. I pick one. It's like Hawaii with a meandering stream. There's a dark bank behind one side of the stream, and there's a bodhisattva, right there, sitting there just perfectly. We can get in the water....we got in the water. No, it's the perfect temperature....

Wow, and there are trees and fruit. The river is winding towards the central peak.... the mountain. We can see it with our mind's eye. *[We don't "travel" up the river, but we're able to "see" as if we travel all the way up and notice and incredible amount of detail all the way, but it all happens in a flash.]* It's gorgeous, and we're getting out of the water and sitting on the bank. It's a sandy bank right at the foot of this diamond, Buddha-like figure in a lotus position, and it's just stunning because you can see through his body. It's like he's made out of clear crystalline material..... he contains so much energy!

SML: What does he represent to you?

M: He represents the overarching God. God crystallized down into this figure that looks like a human. So peaceful, sitting calm and still, and there is energy moving in and around that figure who is 10 or 15 or 20 feet high on a volcanic wall. So that's part of what we're going to talk about. It's so amazing to just sit with these entities like my guide. It's so vast, so much energy. For my guide to appear in this little guy, like my little buddy is just a generous act because his energy is so, so vast compared to that. Wow, I'm very humbled, and it is such an honor .....and this is just my guide!! (Overcome with emotion). And God is 10 trillion times more than that..... It's like they're just trying to cure me of my arrogance. Wow. So the big God, the figure of Crystal on the wall is like my guide and me merged into one. Like Russian nesting dolls, so I got into my guide and my guide got into me on different levels and each one of those bodies has billions of nesting dolls inside of it, like the microcosm in the macrocosm and it's just energy. Every small one is a replication of the big one. They are all linked. They are all the same energy yet different. They are scaled. That's what they're showing me. Now I'm experiencing more on the micro scale, one little particle of life, a very small living entity swimming around. It's like I'm an amoeba or protozoa swimming in the body of one of the smaller scale Buddhas that is the body of a bigger Buddha. And those are just the cells in between the outer shells of the nesting dolls......and the single-celled animal is incredible! It's unbelievable, amazing - the miraculousness of all the scales and the aggregation of energy into all forms, not only the living forms, but also the crystalline forms like the sand and the rock. It's amazing. If you had to give it a human purpose or name, you would call it love, too. It's supporting everything else around it. It's contributing to its welfare. It's all, not just interdependent, but inter-everything! It's like God's idea.

SML: What a wonderful gift to be shown that and have that experience.

M: Now I'm getting back on the sandy beach sitting next to another guide who is now a separate entity as opposed to the unified entity. The arrangement feels like I'm sitting at the feet of the master. I'm asking this guide to help me and teach me. She is such a strong authority but also so loving. I asked her what her name is, and she said it was Heron or something.

SML: Can you ask Heron what your soul name is?

M: She says I have many names. It's not important.

SML: Can you ask Heron what the significance is of the experience you just had?

M: It was an incredible gift to be shown what I was shown. It's like a preview.

SML: So is it appropriate to ask your questions now? Do you still want to ask?

M: Yes, (*with enthusiasm first, then with conviction*) yes.

SML: So your first question is: What do I need to be shown, or what do I need to know right now, at this point in my soul's journey?

M: I'm being shown everything...... I should be in a state of prayer and meditation 24 – 7, but I just need to know that wherever I am and whatever I am doing, I just need to be this light that I am. Let things unfold.... They are appropriate..... just whatever comes up, it's not about personal accomplishment or achievement. It's not about having or doing. It's not about anything like that. It's about going with grace and humility and giving unconditionally like I always want to do anyway. What I need to be shown is this experience, and that's what I need to show to others when the opportunity presents itself. I don't have to seek it, or create it, but when these opportunities occur everywhere, all the time in different settings, on different scales, I need to show this grace, humility, and unconditional giving. The main word I'm getting is trust. To trust the feelings I get and the intuitions, and when things come up I need to slow down and pay attention. And when you get an answer, trust it, don't second guess it. Just get out of the way. Free the self of the preconditions and preconceptions and cultural conditioning, and acknowledge it and love it for what it is, but don't let that override the message. Let it come to the mind from the heart and through the intuition.

SML: Your next question is: Should I be doing anything different to align with my soul's purpose?

M: It's just to love, and that's it. I mean to love .... Language really slows us down, but part of it is love is stronger when there is pain involved, like when it's not reciprocated or when there's pain or perceived danger or whatever. That's when it's really needed. That's when it's really powerful. That's real love. Like when you're safe and all that, is love too, but the sense of separation and the pain and all that I've experienced and others have experienced, is just to make the love stronger, more complete, more true, more expansive, and I'm getting a message that's something like, "Trust in the love of God that is in you." It sounds miniscule in words. When you encounter other people's pain and how that manifests as violence or aggression and fear, and you love them, that's when you really need love, and I've got it. That's what I do. What you need is to let go of all the fear and let go of all the pain in you, and then you are not competing and you know you are on your soul's journey and living your purpose - when you are that pure love that you are. Just trust in the love that you are, and you're always living your purpose and on your path.

SML: Your next question is: What lesson should I be working on now?

M: What I got was, slow down. Love more. All the other stuff you're doing…… just balance that trusting feeling, deeply connecting continuously with this love that you are and the infinite endless eternal energy that everything is made of. If a human emotion comes up, just remember that and rest and do whatever you need to do and feel the connection with that.

Knowledge is expansive and true, and all the other little pains and fears are okay, but that's not the primary reality.

[A better way to explain the message I received in the session with rational mind language, after the fact, is that I was shown that it would be good for me to be compassionate, have empathy for others, feel love, and give love in service to others, but also, if it is tiring or draining, or not working fast enough or well enough for my impatient, arrogant nature, I should give myself permission to rest in the infinite energy of the whole cosmos and reconnect with that feeling in myself - in my own body, mind, and emotions. The primary reality is the energy of all-that-is over eternity. The emotions, thoughts, beliefs, and even the actions and doing are a smaller, and more temporary subset of that.]

It's interesting that the sense I just got is that fake humility is arrogance. They're telling me don't do fake humility as that is arrogance. Instead, be the power that you are, and be the loving way for good.

Healing from Past Life as Mongolian Warrior

SML: You only have one more question on your list that hasn't already been answered: Am I holding any other energy from past lives that I would benefit from releasing, and if so, may I have help in releasing it?

M: I feel something in my throat. Wow! This is more of a feeling of something coming up from my gut. I'm feeling it in my body before I get the image, but it's a release, and I'm getting it right now. I'm asking my guide if I need a conscious reminder of this lifetime to help me release this. Now it's going up into my brain stem, and it's still stuck in my throat. Whoa! It's like an energetic being inside of me that's moving up and trying to move out. It's clinging, especially to the roof of my mouth and my brain stem and the top of my spine, but it's starting to move out. They're moving it out. I have the sense that my guide and other forces are getting rid of this for me. Now it's getting to the core of my brain. I'm seeing if I'm getting a memory. It doesn't feel like it needs to. It's still moving out. I need to work with this. Trust….. it's about trust - trust that it's really being released, really letting go. Just trust. Select your level of trust. My guide says, "Trust me." I say, "Of course I trust you!" I'm the one that's holding it, and I'm trying to let it go. It's like it's evaporating off my skin. I'm honoring it and thanking it, but asking it to go. That wasn't me, but… right now it seems more helpful for me to just feel it. Feel that feeling. There's a shape in the density to it, and it's becoming more and more diffused and evaporating. Its connection into my body is less and less.

SML: Can you trust to let it all go?

M: Some came back to my throat just then.

SML: Ask your guide to help you. Trust your guide to help you.

M: (*in a serious voice*) I was beheaded in one of my lives. My guide is saying that it will be released, but I have to practice this for a little while longer, but not that long. Just a couple months or something, and it will all be released.

SML: Do you need to know anything more about that lifetime that would be helpful to put it in perspective?

M: "Fearful human, Mike" is trying to avoid revisiting this lifetime, but my guide says, yes, let's go into this lifetime. I was a warrior, and I thought I was on the right side of the war. This is an extreme example of trying to force others to do what you think is right through violence and aggression and domination. They made an example of my death. I was a general or a king. I find this kind of repulsive to my "current self".....if my "current self" exists, but I mean this consciousness. After the moment of my death and the time around my death, the spirit really lingered around. My spirit lingered around to see the whole spectacle of my head paraded around. It was belittled and defamed and just beaten and kicked around until there was no skin left on the face. I was reviled, dehumanized and hated. Even though I was primarily good, except for killing other people for what I thought was for good. My spirit needed to see all that in order to get the full effect of the incongruity of what I believed I was doing versus the real reality.

SML: Did you come away with that understanding?

M: No, I was really mad and I still am. Not that much, but still a little bit. The anger and the righteousness was not all burned out, it was still there. And I still held onto a lot of that righteous indignation that hasn't all melted away. It was a big battle, and it was very foolish stuff for me to think one side was more right than the other. It's absurd. I feel it less already in my throat.

SML: Putting it in proper perspective will help you let it go. Trust your guide to help you release that.

M: It took me quite a while after that lifetime to clear out enough so I could see the Council.

SML: What else can help you?

M: My guide is telling me to trust my higher nature, but not the more base impulses. They're saying it in a much more beautiful way. Not the human stuff, but more the spirit stuff like my intuition, and my intention is correct and pure, but then I got caught up in the power over others instead of power with others, and I got away from the pure cooperation and the good of all, and I went more toward domination and the benefit of one side versus the other. It was a big kingdom. *[I was fighting for our kingdom.]* I thought I was acting on behalf of the greater good but it was not for the **greatest good of all**. *[Including other kingdoms.]* So I lost sight of the "of all." I was corrupted by the greed, power and fear. I started out with feelings of love and desire to help and protect others, and then I let the fear and greed take over because I had the desire for power. I was deluding myself at the time, thinking that I was doing it for good, and it took me a long time to clear that out. It's the whole arrogance thing….. the righteous indignation is just another form of violence that does not honor the good of all, so my guide is telling me to just keep in mind that when you serve, it has to serve the good of all. This is your guidance in every moment and every situation. It includes whoever is right in front of you. It's not an abstract concept. In a way, it seems so simple, but I lost track of that in that lifetime. So she's saying trust your intuition and instinct, but just remember to make sure it is for the good of all.

I thank this guide for that information and for sharing that with me also, and I am told that I am welcome.

SML: You have no more questions that you have given me, but are there any more that you would like to ask now? Or perhaps your guide would like to share something else with you.

M: My guide is saying to thank you deeply, like I was flippant in the way I said it, but that's not how it's coming from the guide. She says to thank you very deeply for doing this work and for helping me to get this guidance this time on this journey. My guide says that you're doing what you're supposed to do on your journey, and it's very beautiful, and they are very grateful for you.

SML: Tell her I am very honored to be doing it. Thank you. What else can she tell you right now?

M: My guide is telling me that she's always with me. All I need to do is pay attention. Ask and you shall receive. Listen and you'll hear. Pay attention and I am there. It's very direct. Just shift your attention, it's not even "ask," the guide is always there and always open. All you have to do is shift to that channel; turn the dial to that channel. Listen, ask and listen. Just feeling the energy is helpful for me rather than trying to turn it into language and words that I have to convey to someone else. I can just feel it. And that's a lot faster, especially over the next short period when I am completely releasing all this fear, lack of trust and all that. And when I'm releasing, just feel the energy and feel the transformation and trust it and you'll be feeling it, and it will continue at a very accelerated rate compared to normal. That's another gift that I'm receiving right now is that the transformation can happen very quickly. Just feel the energy and don't try to relate it to anything historical or the past or the future. It's like the next couple months (I've heard this twice now) is the time for me to release this and to just trust it and feel it. And I will remember exactly how to do that. I can just tune into the "guide channel," and it'll help me feel it.

Life Selection

SML: Is there anywhere else you'd like to go, perhaps the place where you select your upcoming lives?

M: Yes. But let me ask. Yes, my guide will take me there. (*after a moment*) We could've gone slowly, but no, we're there. It's like a cylindrical chamber that goes up. I can't see the limit of it. It seems brighter at the top - with light on the top. The bottom is darker, and you can go anywhere you want and select different consoles. There are consoles that you can look at, and the guide, my guide, took me there. And then....... I'm just so dazzled by this that I'm having a hard time focusing my attention on who is with me. I know my guide took me there, and it seems like there's another guide or two there that are helping us. I am trying to try to pay attention to it all. I'm like the kid in the candy store again, and I'm having a hard time focusing...

SML: Do you make the decision yourself, or is it a group decision?

M: You make it yourself ....It's not self really, I don't know if there even really is a self. It's like we are merged with the guides and in the guidance, all the way up, and all the way down, but there is an aspect of individual choice involved. I guess you could say no, but you wouldn't dream of saying no. I trust them up there. There is an aspect of individual choice involved. (Laughs) It's kind of like you could say they're convincing you because they are really patient, so they give you the impression that you are choosing. But they really are choosing what they know to be best for you. They're kind of settling me down right now....getting the kid in the candy store to settle down, and they're showing me, and I'm trying to look at consoles. I start to look at other consoles, but they are guiding me to the right level, the right region and giving me kind of a glimpse of the other ones, but they're really showing me the next life. It's like they are very patient because I keep saying, "Would it work if I do this or I do that," and then they give me a glimpse of other screens or consoles. You can say they're like screens, but you can watch a simulation of that world and that life and it's three dimensional, so you have glimpses of experiences, but they explain it to you.

Just because you see these scenes, it doesn't mean it's guaranteed to happen. There are so many interconnected things happening all the time. So if this thing happens, another thing will happen. It's like they are giving you examples of things that may happen in the different lifetimes, but it's just giving you a feel for it. But you get a really good sense of the general capabilities of that body and the mind, the intuition and all the senses beyond the normal five, and also the body's innate ability versus developing ability. And some of the other types.... It is not like they're taking other souls from your group, but soul types, like the antagonist or the compatible one and you know there are going to be some helpful ones. I guess you do know a few members of the soul groups who are going to be in this life with you. I'm getting that really clearly. (*After a pause*) They're like ....okay, this is really incredible because I'm being shown multi-dimensionally, not just one instance of this, but many instances of this. I can only see a dozen simultaneously because that's all my brain can hold at the moment. Usually they really encourage you to take this one, even if you're too dim to pick it, but sometimes they give you a choice of two or three. Sometimes it could be even more like four or five, but usually it's two or three. And any one is equally okay. It's like any of these two or three would be roughly the same. Then they lay out the elements because we like having variety in the selection, but it really is pretty much aligned to growth and linear evolution.

SML: And one that you may not choose. Is that available to you another time?

M: No, the lifetimes are never the same twice. You can't pick a lifetime later on if you don't pick it now, because lifetimes are never the same twice. You can pick a certain type of profession, or type of body, but all the conditions are different, even if it's in the same country. Let's say you wanted to be a Tibetan Lama one time. Well, that option will be available to you and could be available to you in the future, but it won't be the same. It would appear differently. The teachings will be different. The teachings to the soul group would be different. The particular evolutionary chain would be different. So that's important because your purpose, your small-scale purpose, will overlap with the cultural purpose and humanity's evolutionary purpose, and the timing of those are important. You might be really curious about a Tibetan Lama, but it just might not be right for you at a given time.

SML: What about choices of time periods, different times in history?

M: Let me see. Are you saying can I go back in time or forward in time in my choices?

SML: Yes. How does that work?

M: This is way more interdimensional than one can conceive of it. You might choose a life that's 100,000 years in the future or 100,000 years in the past or on another planet, a totally different evolutionary progression on a different planet and it may seem primitive or advanced but …..There is kind of like a linear thread for your experience, but when you go like from this lifetime, I might go into a lifetime that may seem more primitive.

It's not clear to me from my perspective right now if it's 100,000 years in the future or 100,000 years in the past or another planet.

SML: So you don't choose based on that anyway, just on the life itself.

M: You choose the life itself. It is definitely .... karma is not........... I'm not getting into that.

SML: Have you chosen a life on another planet?

M: Oh, yeah. I have chosen life on another planet. Many times.

SML: Very often?

M: Let me see. This is some wild stuff. This is like time and space is turned inside out. I can see it a little bit, but I can't comprehend it really. It doesn't even make sense to say this planet or other planets because in a way it's all like simulated projection, but you could say that other planets are nested inside this planet, and this planet that we think of as being for human beings in this century are nested inside other planets. So it's just like going to another layer and that's just the way it's being shown to me. That's even not accurate, but it's the only way my Mike mind can comprehend. But it is way more multidimensional than humans talk about now in this century. In a way the current level of human understanding is very primitive - for many of us....most of us, it's all relative.

SML: The last time you were in the selection area how many choices did you have?

M: I just had one choice and this one was it. I mean, I thought I had other choices. They let me shop around. Marie was going to be here (Mike's wife in his current life), and my mom was going to be here, and to be here right now it's very exciting. It's a very exciting time for this planet and this population for the evolution of this collective consciousness manifesting in the beings that are here right now. This is exciting. This is a very exciting time for this planet.

SML: Tell me more about that.

This Planetary Era

M: It is the end of one era and the beginning of another. It is a gradual thing over a long time period. It will take more than just one lifetime, but it's the beginning of a cycle. We are getting more back to the other... going back to the garden and toward harmony and cooperation.

We're pretty much at the peak of war and destroying the earth and all that. This is the worst it's going get. I don't know from my little perspective, but it is like an alcoholic bottoming out. This is hitting bottom, and it might get a little worse before it gets better, but basically the getting better is already happening parallel with the bottoming out. So getting better is rising up big right now, real big. Wow! And it's beautiful like a beautiful flower, the uplift part. Even with all the scary stuff, it's beautiful. This human life is that in the microcosm.

[This matches Joseph Rael's "fifth world" but seems inaccurate and hard to believe in 2019 with the 45th president and even globally with all of the political, cultural, and ecological problems and challenges...]

SML: For those who have chosen to be here now?

M: That is why a lot of us are here now.... for the uplift part. This human life is that *[transformation]* in microcosm.

SML: Ask your guide how best can we help this all along?

M: Each in our own way. There is no one answer for everyone, but we know it when we feel it.

Simplicity really, every choice, every step, every breath is to serve the greatest possible good, and the self is included in that.

You don't have to live in poverty or be homeless on the street to be part of the greatest good, but you don't need more than you need either. I don't know how else to say it. Wow. That's so amazing, that even just my guide...... oh, I don't mean to say it disparagingly...... every guide is a channel for infinite wisdom like this, and each of us are.

SML: Anything else important to know?

M: This life was pretty much created for me as an ideal match. I wasn't allowed too much arrogance – not too handsome or ugly, not too strong or weak, not too healthy or sick, but there's still great capacity there, and it's a beautiful gift. But it took me a long time to realize that.

SML: Or maybe you don't have too much arrogance anymore?

M: (laughs) Oh, I still have a fair amount. (smiles)

SML: Anything else your guide has to say about this?

M: My guide is telling me, or showing me, that I don't really need these antagonistic, tricky, angry sneaky lessons anymore. I don't need to choose those, and she's telling me to go with the uplifted, the light, high ....higher companions and influences that are around as opposed to the darker ones. In this lifetime ... right now. And that will help with the trust thing and with my life's work - with the "all" that is me. Go with the light beings. Thank the others, bless them and honor them, but let them go on their journey. Don't try to change them or fix them. It's like the same lesson over and over. How many times do I have to get it? But it is true this lifetime as well. So my guide says, go ahead, go back.

SML: Are you sure you're ready?

M: Yes.

I suggest that Mike be guided back into his body, and I add my suggestion that this beautiful world is always accessible. He arrives back in his body and is brought to full waking consciousness with a complete memory of everything he experienced.

Comments on the LBL regression

I found the loving, playful, wise energy of the guide, the soul groups, the council, and the life selection helpers amazing! That experience transformed and healed me in this lifetime. I am calmer and more at ease now. I don't feel that I only live once. I feel this life is part of a bigger unfoldment.

I still feel trauma in the throat and am still learning to trust. It wasn't a magic bullet, or instant fix. But it was probably a 99% solution. I feel I am almost "home free", but not quite there yet. Or, I can say I get lots of moments and even stretches of peace, joy, and fulfillment where I know and feel in the body and emotions, perfectly OK, with no struggle, fear, striving, or doubt. But, I still have the human neurotic patterns playing along some as well.

The main lessons were about letting go of my judgment and arrogance; learning and accepting the fact that other people make their own choices and follow their own paths; trusting in my own goodness, wisdom, and divinity; and remembering to always serve the good of all in even the smallest and simplest of ways. I am also humbled, and empowered by the gift and honor of the images of interconnectedness and the sense that all scales of being are made of the "same stuff". Also, the idea that the guide, or guides, and council, are always available is very comforting. In my case, the rational, thinking, analyzing mind is very strong though, and I have to really concentrate to relax and get quiet enough to sense this kind of partnering guidance and intelligence. The chattering, busy, "rational" mind is still active, and experiencing the subtle energetic presence and guidance of spirit is still intermittent but emerging and occurring more frequently.

Past Life as Chokrel

During the past-life regression hypnotherapy session in October 2015, which was part of the preparation for the Life Between Life session that followed, this life came up. In the hypnotherapy session, this life was just a brief sketch.

In the months that followed, I was interested in knowing more about an early lifetime, any lifetime. So, on March 11th, 2017, I did my own deep meditation with a sequence like the past life hypnotic regression session. I wanted to see if I could do a "self-hypnosis-like" regression. I had the intention of "journeying" into a lifetime and letting spirit bring up whatever would be most helpful and illuminating. It worked and the lifetime from the earlier session came up again. As I got into it the middle of it, I had requests to explore specific topics and questions in more detail. For the most part, whatever I wanted to know about was shown to me. But, a few times, it wasn't. The self-hypnosis lasted 2 to 3 hours and provided amazing detail which I was able to recall completely.

I started the deep meditation / self-hypnosis by calming myself to clear the mind. I focused on the breathing during this part. It lasted several minutes. Then, when I felt calm, I started counting breaths. I started with my then current age of 54, and counted down and moved backward in time 1 year of my life per breath. I also visualized going down stairs – one stair per count. The stairs started off at ground level and went down underground toward a door. I stopped at a few key ages to experience moments in the current life.

I "saw" or "was "immersed in a scene" where Mom taught me to pray for her and practice connecting with my angelic self when I was about two years old. When I was that age, many emotionally impactful things happened for my Mom. Within the previous year, her dad, John Torres, plus our grandpa Teodocio Martinez (my Dad's Mom's Dad who lived next door and was a benefactor to the family), and a baby she miscarried, all died. She was emotionally wrung out. My Dad provided emotional support to her, up to a point. As the little toddler I was, I devotedly followed her around and helped her too. I asked her if she was OK. One day she was lying in bed and feeling low and I asked "Are you OK Mama?" She said she was having a hard time and she needed to rest. I asked if I could help her or do anything for her. She said I could pray for her. I asked her how. She told me to kneel at the side of her bed and put my hands in a prayer posture by my heart and ask God to help her. So I did it. I was in nearly pure angelic form then, so my prayers were very powerful and pure. She reminded me and showed me that I was her guardian Angel just like she was my Guardian Angel.

When I regressed to my birth, at countdown zero, I was at the bottom of the stairs and I paused in front of a doorway and asked to feel the presence of my guide

The doorway was shaped like a vesica piscis with two halves that opened to the sides:

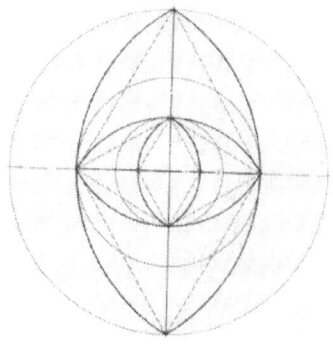

My guide met me – her/his name was/is Astara.
I asked the guide if I could explore my first humanoid/Earth lifetime.
The guide conveyed telepathically that I should "take it slow", "be patient" and not try to take in too much.
I (impatiently) said "OK. So, can we go now!"
The guide said yes.

The Past Life – 80,000 years ago

I looked down at my body – I was a male, short (about 5'0" tall, or maybe 5'2", max). I was lean, athletic, and hairy. I asked where we were and when it was. I was told in the Alps (by modern day Germany), 80,000 years ago. I realized it was the same life from the earlier past life regression hypnotherapy session. I asked to be shown whatever I should be shown. But I had a couple of specific requests: I wanted to know if any of the people in that lifetime were in my current lifetime – especially my spouse, parents, children, and close friends, family, and teachers from that lifetime…

Asara's death

I was taken straight to my wife's deathbed. I wanted to know more about her. I telepathically asked my guide and my guide let me "know" all the following: Her name was "Asara" (uh-SAW-ruh). She was 10 years younger than me. We became mates when she was about 14 years old and I was about 24. She died when she was about 25 (I was around 35), so we were together as mates for about 11 years. We had 4 children together. The 3 oldest were girls aged 10, 8, and 7. Our son was the youngest, about 4 years old, when she passed. She died in childbirth with our fifth child. The baby died too.

~~~~~~~~~~~~~~~~~

Next, the deathbed scene unfolded. There were 3 midwives helping her. They tried to save her, but when Asara and the baby died, the midwives cleaned them up, wrapped them up, then called me in to see them. I was nervous and pacing around outside the hut until they called me in. When the elder midwife called me in, she said "Chokrel (my name in this lifetime), come see this!" The way she said it I thought I was going to see my wife and new baby in perfect health.

But, when I went into the hut, Asara and the stillborn baby were clean and wrapped, but lying still on the bed and they were DEAD! I was shocked and saddened but it was all OK, because the spiritual light bodies of Asara, our baby and our Mother (who had passed away 5 years earlier) were standing behind and to the side of the dead bodies!

The spirit form Asara was holding our baby in her arms and our Mother was right next to them. Asara told me "I'm alright, our baby's alright, Mom's right here with us, and you will be alright too – whatever you do." I understood this to mean that they were wonderful in Spirit form on the other side and that whatever was coming up for me on the Earth from here on for the rest of my life would be OK too. I "knew" they (Asara, my Mom, and our baby) were my spirit allies and they would be around to guide, protect, comfort, and console me and our surviving children through the rest of our Earthly lives.

It was an amazing miracle to see this. The elder midwife, Rasana, could see these spirits too. I wasn't sure, but it seemed like the other two midwives were able to feel something powerful and beautiful there too. But I don't think they were able to "see" and hear all of it like Rasana and I. Somehow I knew both Rasana and I had the same experience.

~~~~~~~~~~~~~~~~~

Even with the amazing vision and comforting messages from the departed ones, I was numb for a while. I was in shock. I couldn't believe what had just happened. Death at childbirth happened quite often in our tribe, but I didn't expect it now, with Asara. For a few days I walked around in a daze and haze. I couldn't function. I was a wreck. I didn't eat or sleep. I couldn't think clearly or understand anything. I was struck.

Our children were asking for their Mama, saying they were hungry, and things like that.

The village was very sophisticated about things like this. Everyone pitched in and sprang into action. Some village members took care of the kids. Some villagers helped prepare the burial and death ceremonies. Some villagers supported me in my grieving.

There was a custom in the village that when a death happened in the family, those affected could step away from the normal village duties and responsibilities for a whole month (one cycle of the moon). During this month, the grieving person, or people would be supported, continuously. They had someone available to them at all times. They always had someone to talk to and walk with. They weren't left alone. They also had meals and other living comforts provided by the community. They had continuous nurturing and comforting support for a whole lunar cycle. It was a very enlightened "family leave plan". The month-long timeframe was a loose guideline and not a strict requirement. If people wanted to move into their routines quicker or slower, it was OK. But if it extended much beyond a month, there was increasing communal pressure for the grieving person to "get back into their life". This was a beautiful system for everyone involved – both the givers and the receivers.

After several days, the burials were complete, the most severe shock and numbness wore off, and Chokrel became angry, sad, and worried with feelings of guilt. Chokrel was a good husband and father. He was completely devoted and enjoyed his wife and children. He had never been mean, or abusive, or irresponsible. But he felt guilty because he felt he had not expressed his appreciation to Asara enough when she was alive. He took her for granted sometimes and didn't always show or tell her how much she meant to him and how much he loved her. He thought she probably knew, but he still felt bad about it. If he would've known she was leaving then, he would've let her know he loved and appreciated her more.

Chokrel went on walks by the river and in the woods. He talked with his friends and visited and played with his kids every day. But, he was in his "grieving time", so he didn't take care of his kids. He didn't know how to take care of little kids and he didn't have patience, and he was an emotional wreck.

His kids kept asking for their Mom and he had to explain that her spirit left her body and she wouldn't be coming back. Some of the kids couldn't understand or accept it. He explained that it was like when a tree falls, it doesn't get back up, or grow again out of the roots. Or when their pets died, they were gone and didn't come back. Or it was like when the fish, birds, or other animals, and plants they ate stopped living and breathing, they never came back either. Chokrel told the kids their Mama and the baby were spirits that were still alive, just not in the body anymore and when that happened, the bodies stopped being alive for good.

Rasana (ruh-SAW-nah)

The elder midwife, Rasana, was also a medicine woman and she was involved in the burial ceremonies.

After the burials, about a week after the deaths, Rasana offered to take care of Chokrel and Asara's four kids for the grieving Moon period. Chokrel agreed.

Everyone agreed that Rasana would take care of the kids in their parent's (Chokrel and Asara's) hut. It was less traumatic for the kids that way and easier for Rasana. But it was taboo for Chokrel to be there with Rasana. So he spent time with other friends and out in nature.

The tribe had a taboo against immediate pair bonding after the loss of a mate. The expected "normal" waiting time before finding another mate was about 1 year. This was a flexible guideline. Sometimes people would find new mates in 3 moons, 6 moons, 9 moons, or even years later, and of course some never took new mates. Pairing up as rapidly as 4 or 5 moon months was somewhat frowned upon. 6 or 7 moon months was somewhat questioned, like "Are you sure it's not too soon? There's no hurry." But, 9 or 10 months to a year or more was considered OK. No questions asked or challenges raised.

Chokrel had wonderful support and transformational release during his month of grieving. He saw his kids every day and was grateful for Rasana's help. He was able to spend a lot of his time re-"viewing" his life with Asara and his love for her. He felt great appreciation for their relationship and time together.

At the end of the one month grieving period, Chokrel decided he wanted to move back in to his hut and be with his kids. He also wanted to get back to his fishing, hunting and gathering duties with his male compatriots, but he didn't know how to do both. He asked Rasana for advice because if he was in the hut with his kids, she couldn't be there too. It was taboo.

She said it would be OK for her to stay in the family hut as long as their conduct was pure. Rasana was a respected elder on the council. She was a medicine woman, midwife, and healer. She was a "seer" too. She was psychic. She said she knew this question and request was likely to come up and she had already bounced the idea off the council. They were open to Rasana living in Chokrel's hut to take care of the four children as long as there was no pair bonding conduct between Rasana and Chokrel.

When she told Chokrel, he was surprised it was OK with the council, but he happily accepted it.

They did not seem like pair bonding material anyway. Rasana was about 15 years older than Chokrel. He was about 35. She was about 50. He was a healthy prospect in his near-peak years. He was well regarded as a physically and emotionally strong, dependable, open-hearted and even-tempered character. He was a catch and there were even several women his age and younger he could probably pair with. Rasana was patient, and kind, but somewhat reclusive and mysterious. Plus, she was somewhat plain looking. Not quite unattractive, just "plain" looking. She was an "old maid" who had a reputation for never having wanted a pair-bonding relationship with a man. So, the community thought it was safe.

At the end of the first month with both Chokrel and Rasana in the hut together with the children, they decided to continue for another month, then another...

Over time, Chokrel realized he had a deep respect for Rasana's temperament and her selfless, loving, kind generosity with the children. After 3 or 4 months, Chokrel began thinking maybe he should mate with Rasana. She felt it too. They talked and were both cautiously positive about the prospect. But, they remained pure in their private and public conduct.

After 6 months, or so, they were always together, even in social settings and they appeared in the community as a couple in every way except physical intimacy. At that point, they pretty much knew they wanted to become a mated pair. But, they waited a few more months before putting feelers out in the community. At about 9 months, they started putting the word out. And after a year, they tied the knot with the blessing of the community. Many women were sad about this one that got away. But the community greatly respected and appreciated both of them, their young family, and their whole family unit that had developed.

Rasana was a wonderful mother to Chokrel and Asara's children. Chokrel and Rasana did not have any children together. In fact, their relationship was more of a helping and learning partnership than a romantic, physical relationship. It's not clear they even consummated their relationship at all, and if they did, the physical aspect of their relationship was more about healing, mutual support, and comfort than raw and wild lust, passion, and sexual urges.

During the regression, I asked my guide, Astara, to show me more about Rasana.

It turns out that Rasana had been around for Chokrel and Asara's whole life. She was like a babysitter for Chokrel and

Asara when they were younger. And Rasana was also a friend and student of Chokrel's mother. She had always been in the close inner circle of Chokrel's life, but Chokrel had always considered her to be kind of a Spiritual Aunt. He had never considered her a potential mate until he saw her with his kids in his house those few months after Astara's death.

Chokrel and Rasana had many good years together.

Rasana had been Chokrel's mother's primary student her whole life and now Chokrel was able to continue learning the medicine/healing/spiritual work from Rasana.

For many years, up until about age 42, Chokrel continued to work with the men fishing, hunting, telling stories, trapping and collecting. But around age 42, it became clear to Chokrel that he wanted to spend more, then most, and ultimately all, of his working time with Rasana. They became a powerful team. They supported, pushed and pulled each other but they were also a tremendous asset to the community. They were the principle medicine people. They facilitated physical, emotional, ceremonial, and community cooperation and harmony both in times of celebration and in circumstances of conflict and crisis.

The kids grew older. The two older daughters mated, and had families. The youngest daughter and their son were still in the parent's home. But they were all doing great.

Rasana died around age 63 when Chokrel was about 48. This was a VERY old age for this community. But, she knew a lot about health and wellness, which helped her survive a long time in wonderful health and die a relatively painful and easy death. She was well loved by all and closed out her relationships and Earthly life in the body with great grace and dignity.

It was a lot easier for Chokrel to move through the emotions of Rasana's death than it had been with Asara. Largely because Rasana foresaw it and gently prepared him as the time approached. Also, it was easier for him than Asara's loss because he was older and more mature, and their relationship and time and work together had more of a feeling of "completeness". Social factors made it easier too. He had fewer responsibilities, less worries, and more time to grieve and delve deeper into meaningful connection with the cosmos, and productivity in the community than he had when he was younger when Asara died. He had a wonderful fullness and closure before Rasana's death that he hadn't quite had with Asara.

As it turned out, there was lots of contact with Asara and Rasana after their deaths, so the ongoing relationship was more of a continuity of connection than a closure or end. Their relationships extended beyond the physical forms.

My Mothers

I wanted to know more about my upbringing with my mother.

I was shown that I was brought up by an incredibly kind, patient, loving, giving mother. She was a midwife, medicine woman, herbalist, energy worker, and council elder

But she was not my birth mother! [We'll circle back and get more about her in a sec...]

My Birth Mother

My birth mother died at my birth

I asked to know more about my birth mother and I was shown that she was a very pure person – amazing! But she was young – maybe 14 and became pregnant when she was raped by her father. My birth father was also my grandfather.

Rape and incest were taboo in this society. My birth mother and her mother protected the father/husband/rapist because they didn't want him to be punished and possibly banished from the community. They were in a tough bind. If they reported him, they'd probably be sending him away forever, but if they didn't, they'd have to live with him and possibly endure more misconduct. And either way the young mother would most likely be blamed, shamed, and shunned.

I tried to see more about this rapist father/grandfather and the complicit grandmother, but I was not shown much. I was allowed to "know" that he was mostly "out of the picture" and he was not a factor in young Chokrel's life. But, that's all I needed to know. It was conveyed to me that knowing any more details about them would not be helpful to me, so I would not be shown any more.

I was instructed to unplug all that dark energy from my soul and release it by burning it in a violet flame. My spirit Guide and I did that and watched all that karma release.

System of Justice for Transgressions

I was shown that this community had a sophisticated system for taking care of violations of tribal taboos.

First of all, everyone was taught what was and was not OK in the community. This was taught in the home and in the extended village family and teaching structures from a very young age and throughout life.

Murder was not tolerated. Neither were sexual improprieties such as rape and incest. Violence, assault, coercion, lying, cheating, and stealing were also grave offenses.

This was a VERY peaceful, harmonious, mutually supportive community, so there weren't many big problems, but disputes and passions did arise all the time.

Serious transgressions were rare – maybe one every two or three years. But resolution of disputes and disagreements, plus minor infractions deemed worthy of council and community level intervention happened fairly often – around once a month.

The procedure for addressing these violations had multiple steps:
- First, the accusation was brought to the council. This was usually in confidence.
- The council would discuss the strategy to resolve the issue.
- Council members would work with the accused and the accuser through private and joint mediation.
- If the issue was significant enough, the accused would have to appear before the whole council. Sometimes the accuser or accusers were included and sometimes the proceedings would happen in front of the whole village – depending on how much "collective energy" was thought to be best to restore harmony. But, sometimes there would be closed council meetings in private with just the accused.
- First the offender would be honored, acknowledged, praised, respected and reminded of his or her value and esteem in the community. People would tell good stories vouching for the character of the accused and ask the accused to please choose to be a harmonious member of the community.
- Then the accused person or persons would be asked to tell their version of the story and how they would like to

proceed to restore harmony for all involved including themselves.
- For serious offenses, this part of the proceeding could last for up to four days with lots of the village participating in the healing and releasing of the offense!
- Next, after the cleansing, if the offense was serious enough, the offender would be banished from the tribal village for a month (one lunar cycle). They would be escorted 10 to 15 miles away from the village by at least 3 strong, adult, male hunter/warriors where they were dropped off with meager provisions of food, clothing, shelter, weapons and tools.
- If the offense rose to this level, it was VERY serious.
- The difficult conditions during the banishment were such that it might be difficult for the person to survive and if they did survive they could be in such a weakened state, that the return journey might be very difficult.
- The period of isolation was intended to be an interval of self-reflection and atonement.
- At the end of the lunar cycle, the offending person chose whether to return to the village or stay away.
- When (or if) they returned, they were given the chance to explain what they learned and how they planned to change their behavior or institute restitution and/or what they would do to restore harmony. They pled their case to return to village life. The village then decided whether to accept them back.
- It was very rare for the village not to forgive them. But occasionally, the village would choose to banish.
- It was also rare for a person to be given a second chance. Usually, the second time someone was sent away, they did not have the option to return.

- A closely held secret was that sometimes, when the warriors took the criminals out for their month away, they actually killed the criminals so they could not return to harm the village again. There were rumors about this but no one but the inner council and the most trusted warriors knew for sure and they were all sworn to secrecy about it.

I suspect my rapist father, and maybe my grandmother suffered this fate.

Also, I suspect my birth mother chose – on a soul level – to die at childbirth so she would not have to deal with the stigma, social isolation, and emotional pain of the circumstances.

But, those circumstances were all part of the karmic fate for those souls.

My Mother Astara who raised me and my soulmate/first love Asara

I was very fortunate, because I was delivered into the care of an incredible "foster Mom" or "Spiritual Mother". She was extraordinary. She was powerful, strong, gentle, kind, wise, patient, loving, fun, peaceful, and generous.

I asked the name of my adoptive Mom and I got "Astara".

I felt her energy and what it was like being around her. She was an extremely loving, protective, patient, and calmly guiding Spirit. I realized she had the same name as my Spirit guide that met me before I regressed beyond my current life. When I checked her energy, I realized she was my Spirit Guide! My Sprit Guide had come into physical form and taken this role of my adoptive Mother to nurture and guide me through my first human incarnation on Earth! This was an extremely generous act. It filled me with tremendous gratitude and humility.

I then quickly got to see that my first wife, Asara, was also raised with me in the same household by our Spiritual Mother.

Asara's birth mother died during her birth as well. Her birth mother was very pure – just like mine - and she died in childbirth too. Asara had a regular father though – unlike me. He was a good man. But, he died soon after Asara was born, when she was about 2 years old.

When Asara became an orphan at age 2, she went to live with Astara and I.

So Asara was my adoptive, foster, orphan sister when we were growing up.

I always thought of her as my sister, not as a potential romantic partner.

But, I always adored her! She was so smart, observant, gentle, peaceful, pleasant, and curious. AND, she was cute as a button.

When we were younger, and I was about 17 and she was about 7, I was expected to take a mate and move into a traditional village male role. A wonderful village girl was arranged to be my partner, but we met, and both decided we didn't "match".

I wanted to be around my Mom and learn healing and medicine work. But I also wanted to do "Men" stuff like fishing and hunting. I was spoiled. I was allowed to do some of both.

Other village girls were available and I was an eligible bachelor, I even met with some of them, but none of them "fit" me, so I wasn't interested.

I continued in this way until I was almost 22.

Up until my early twenties, I figured I would continue to be a part-time fisher, hunter, gatherer, and part-time medicine man.

Something changed when Asara blossomed and became a young woman. Suddenly, I wanted us to become a mated pair. Asara wanted it too. Our mother encouraged it, and we became a bonded pair when she was 14 and I was 24 (ish).

During the hypnosis/regression, I asked if we were twin souls (two souls that created from one). The answer was yes! This was her first life on Earth too, just like me. I was eager to take on the incarnation and have the experience, but she was timid and reluctant. That's why she had waited 10 years to see how I would like it and if Astara was going to be there and the conditions would be right. The universe arranged all this so that we could both be guided by our Spirit guide in incarnate form as brother and sister for a while, then as mates. But, it also happened in a way that didn't violate social customs.

My connection with and Love for Asara was truly the highest, most complete, and pure form of connection possible between two human beings. We were connected in every way – physically, mentally, emotionally, spiritually and we had the highest and deepest regard, care, and concern for each other. We had FUN too! We were soul mates and even twin flames – two souls created from one.

A day in the Life

I asked to be shown a typical day in Chokrel's life and I was shown a day when Asara was still alive and the three girls were born, but not the boy. The girls were around 5, 3 and 2.

Chokrel woke up early and stoked the fire. He enjoyed a little time with Asara and the girls.

Around sunrise, he went down to the river (which was just a few hundred feet away) to gather water for the family. He carried the water in bladders made out of tanned animal skins. He made a few trips and filled up small, clay pot cisterns inside the family hut.

He also gathered some wood for the day as they had fires burning pretty much all the time.

The family had an early-to-mid-morning breakfast together. The meal consisted primarily of a paste-like porridge. It was made out of a starchy root vegetable of some kind. Also, there were bits of other materials in the porridge. Some of the bits had a nut-like flavor and texture. There were also little bits of leaves that gave the concoction flavor. Overall, it had a pleasant, nutty flavor. It was slightly sweet and slightly salty. It tasted kind of halfway between taro chips and wheat thins, but mild… I was curious about the "nuts" so I tried to see more about them. It turns out they were not nuts. They were roasted grubs. These grubs were delicious! They were either eaten raw, lightly roasted, or completely dried out and stored over the winter. They had great nutrition and great flavor – kind of like macadamia nuts, but lighter… Yum!

After a pleasant breakfast with the family, Chokrel met up with a couple of mates to go out beyond the village.

First they went to the river to check their fishing traps. They had pretty elaborate fishing traps. They were made out of basket-like material. Each trap was like a big funnel spreading out across the stream. On the outer edges of the river, there were vertical walls that funneled the fish toward a central basket. The central basket was a net woven out of flexible plant fibers. The design was ingenious. The whole arrangement was made up of small, modular pieces that could each be removed and taken back to the village for repair. The side pieces were maybe a couple of feet wide and attached to vertical poles that were driven into the stream bed. The net was connected to a frame that allowed it to be lifted out whole when it had fish.

These pieces were in need of continuous repair.

Since the river was so close to the village – just a few hundred feet away – it was easy to go to the fish traps, and back to the village fairly quickly. They'd gather fish, do spot repairs at the river, and take any parts of the fish traps that needed more extensive repair back to the village.

The village was roughly divided into two halves. One half focused upstream from the village, the other half focused downstream. This division fostered healthy competition.

They had about 8 to 10 of these fish traps – half upstream and half downstream.

On this day, Chokrel's upstream crew got 3 fish – pretty big ones.

After that, they ventured farther from the village to check their land-based traps they had set out farther down the valley.

They had two types of traps on land: pit traps, and sling traps.

The pit traps were big holes dug in the ground that were covered with branches. They'd put bait on top of the middle of the covering. They'd either use food, like berries, or small pieces of fat or meat, or they'd put some musk scent collected from previous animals. They trapped larger animals in these pits, like archaic deer, boar, and bear.

They had 4 of these pit traps upstream from the village.

On this day, they didn't catch anything in these pit traps, but they refreshed the coverings, and freshened up the musk on top.

For the sling traps, they had little loops of hide rope tied to a bent over tree or a mechanism that would snag or drop a box on the animal to capture it. There were smaller little twigs that would trigger the mechanism. They put bait and musk on these too. These traps were used for smaller game, like rodents, and birds.

They had about 20 of these type traps.

On this day, they caught a rabbit, a squirrel, and a skunk. They couldn't use the skunk, so they took it away from the trap and buried it.

They gave that job to the youngest member of the crew. That was the tradition, and they each had their time in this role at the bottom rung.

They carried tote bags slung around one shoulder. These tote bags were used to carry whatever they captured back to the village. They also carried their tools in there. They had small clubs – to knock out the fish, or animals – they also had stone knives, spears, and small throwing sticks with little leather cups on the ends. The leather cups held small stones. They were extremely proficient with these little, stone-throwing sticks. They practiced with these stone-throwing tools from the time they were little kids. They had contests and target practice as kids. Some of the men were VERY good. All of the men were good with them, but some were extraordinary.

They used the stone-throwing sticks to kill small animals – especially birds. Since they were hunting most of the day, they were in silence a lot of time each day.

On this day, the small troop came upon a flock of large ground birds similar to grouse. One or two guys almost always had their throwing sticks out and loaded up so they were ready to take a shot at any time they encountered game. The best thrower would always have his stick loaded and ready, plus a backup guy. On this day, the lead guy hit one of the large ground birds with a rock and stunned it. The rest of the guys ran up to the bird and killed it with their clubs.

It was a good day: they had 5 fish, 3 small animals, and a largeish bird to take back to the village. It would be a feast tonight.

And it would be interesting to compare their catch with the downstream squad.

The rest of the day, the hunter/gatherer crew hiked farther on the trails and gathered berries, nuts, and plants.

They used the plants for food and medicine. They were very sophisticated in their knowledge and use of these plants. They only used leaves from some plants. Other plants, they used branches, stalks, seeds, and/or roots.

If they used all parts of the plant, instead of plucking the whole plant out, they'd cut about a quarter of it out and leave most of it planted. This way the plant would still be able to grow and they'd have the plant there as a resource in future years.

One time, they had one of these quarter plants lying around on the ground in their village, it rained, and they noticed that the plant started growing more roots and leaves. This gave them the idea to plant it in the ground by their village so they'd have it available close by instead of having to venture far down the valley. They learned they could cultivate plants and began to do so in a rudimentary way.

As the afternoon grew to a close, they headed back to the village to allow time to prepare the food for the evening meal.

They were regaled as conquering heroes each day when they returned.

The whole village was harmonious. All worked together for the mutual benefit of the whole.

They even had an intelligent system for keeping the older people involved in the productivity of the village. The older people stayed in the village during the day and taught the younger ones about the chores they'd be performing as they got older. The older men taught the pre-pubescent and adolescent boys about animals, their habits, the traps, how to dress them (cut them up and prepare the meat), plus how to gather plants, and how to make and use their tools, and do construction and repairs around the village. The elder women taught the young girls about preparing food, cooking, making pottery, taking care of the children, sewing, and preparing medicines. The elders also taught the young ones about village customs and rituals including coming of age and mating. The elders who had lived this wisdom their whole lives, were the teachers of the community and the youth, with their playful energy, enlivened the elders.

Chokrel's Later Life

After Rasana passed over to the spirit world, Chokrel was a full-time elder, teacher, and healer.

The oldest girls had families of their own with wonderful children and mates that Chokrel saw in the village every day.

The son was a great hunter, and trapper with a family of his own.

The youngest daughter stayed home with her father out of concern for his welfare and also to pursue her interest in learning the family vocation.

Chokrel encouraged her to take a mate and have her own family, but she wasn't interested. She wanted to be around her Dad.

Chokrel was given a special elder status in the community. He helped teach the kids, like most elders, but he was allowed lots of freedom to explore on his own, free from normal, formal responsibilities. He was allowed freedom to spend his time exploring, experimenting, and creating new forms and mechanisms of teaching and healing. Nowadays, we'd call what he did in this phase of his life "research".

He spent most days out in nature. Sometimes he gathered medicinal plants, and brought them back to the village for preparation and use in healing. He experimented and learned about new uses and combinations of medicines. But mostly he spent time "feeling" the energy of nature, contemplating, meditating, and praying about the village welfare and the harmony of "All" nature, plants, animals, land, water, sky. (There were no words, or concepts like that back then. But, that's what we'd call it nowadays).

Nature was his greatest teacher and companion.

He remembered his beloved Mothers, wives, children, grandchildren, and he thought, prayed, and performed ceremonies for all the village members all the time.

He remembered the animals and plants and wonderful forces of nature he had experienced.

He gave thanks for all of it.

He was pleased that his youngest daughter had such natural gifts and great love of healing, plants, herbs, and village healing in all forms – physical, mental, emotional, and spiritual. In fact, she had taken over for him and become the village's primary day-to-day medicine woman.

Chokrel was also grateful that she had so faithfully taken care of him in his last years.

I asked to know more about the final day of Chokrel's life since this was something that was shown to me in the earlier past life meditation/hypnotherapy session leading up to my life between life session.

I was shown the same as the previous session:

The day started early for Chokrel. He woke before sunrise and gathered the small pack he had assembled in the days before. The pack had food, water, and ceremonial items – mostly related to the beloved people and memories in his life. He put on layers of clothes, gathered his belongings, and said a loving farewell to his sweet daughter Amara without waking her.

Then he set off far up the valley. He went at a leisurely pace, lovingly enjoying and appreciating everything along the way knowing that it would be the last time he would experience it in this physical and mental form.

In the late afternoon, he got to a high spot where he could see the whole river valley, fields, and surrounding mountains below. It was a transcendentally beautiful spot and experience.

He was at one and he WAS ONE with all of it – the trees, the birds, the insects, the Earth, the Sky, and the People.

He knew this was to be his last day. He had grown old. He had done what he needed to do on the Earth and now he was ready and even EXCITED to reunite with Astara, Asara, Rasana, and the other Spirit/Energy/beings beyond the embodied form.

He had a nice snack, made a comfortable spot, stayed up for a while to watch the stars and moon, then went to sleep to dream the BIG dream where he allowed his consciousness to release from the physical form.

Over time, after his passing, he communicated with the living ones in many ways. They knew he was OK, and he knew they were OK.

Past Life and Life Between Life Summary

These experiences with past lives and the life between lives changed things for me. Afterward, I no longer felt that I had to do it all and get everything right in just one lifetime. Instead, I now had a sense that healing, growth, forgiveness, power, and peace were always in my grasp but the fullness of being is also a process that unfolds over time.

I noticed that there were some threads of continuity across lifetimes. I had some of the same gifts, tendencies, and blind spots from lifetime to lifetime. But, I also was able to move and grow too.

Closing Thoughts

Life is a beautiful mystery that is much grander and more subtle than the mere rational mind can comprehend or articulate.

These experiences that I recount here (along with others that I've left out) have taken me on a journey of remembering who I really am.

I am someone and something much larger than my ego or self-conception. I am more than my body, thoughts, emotions, history, and even imagination. I am more than my family, and cultural background. **I am more than I even know – we all are.**

All of this gives me a great sense of expansive movement compared to any firm, fixed identity that's based on a set of ideas that come from a sphere of experience that's limited to my own personal background or even a historical or cultural background.

Being awake and open to All – even subtle, and non-ordinary reality - as long as it causes no harm, and contributes to the greater good and harmony for all is a guiding principle for me now.

I am grateful for all of it. And I am grateful to share this with you, now.

Made in the USA
San Bernardino, CA
02 April 2019